DAILY DOSE OF REASON

PAUL JOHNSON
DAILY DOSE OF REASON TEAM

Dose of Reason Publishing

Introduction

When we set out to write a book that would make Enlightenment thinking digestible on a daily basis, the prospect excited us. The lessons from the great Enlightenment Era thinkers have had such a profound impact on our lives, we could not wait to share them with others.

Quickly, we realized the task was not as simple as it seemed. Questions emerged.

The first question focused on "**when?**" What time period were we going to define as the Enlightenment? Would we use the more strict definition of the "Long 18th Century," which was ~1685 to ~1815? Or would we use a more relaxed definition of the time period, to include early 17th century philosophers and late 19th century transcendentalists?

Then there was the very relevant question of "**where?**" The Enlightenment occurred gradually in different parts of the world. Which locales would we consider for our Enlightenment influences? Would we contain the geography to the way the Enlightenment reached through Europe and eventually into America, or expand to recognize the earlier influences from Asia and Africa?

Closely tied to the question of *when* is the concept of

what should be included in our definition of the Enlightenment. The Renaissance, Scientific Revolution, Enlightenment, Revolutions in America and France, and the Transcendental Enlightenment of the 19th century America all have strong threads to the broader Enlightenment thinking. It became more difficult than expected to draw a clear line around the Enlightenment Era.

Most importantly, *who* would be the people we include in a snapshot of 365 enlightenment ideas? It was not a decision we took lightly. Obviously, none of the people we write about are alive today to defend themselves or plead their case. The best we could do was select thinkers who were representative of the era in some way, and provided ideas that we thought could still be useful today.

That left us with the question of *how*, which fortunately was a more obvious answer. We wanted to create something for today's reader that was bite-sized. It was important that the book appeal to any reader - not just people who were students of philosophy or history. We wanted to introduce you to some of the people who have influenced not only our thinking, but the direction of humankind over the past few centuries.

Orientation

It is important to give the reader some boundaries and guides on the definitions we landed on for this book.

We chose to expand the time period we used for the passages in this book beyond "The Long 18th Century." It was important to go back to the earlier 1600s to capture the influential thinking of Francis Bacon, Thomas Hobbes, and Rene Descartes – the three earliest-born profiled in this book. Likewise, we decided that we needed to extend beyond the early 1800s and capture some of the American Transcendentalist thinkers like Emerson and Thoreau. The latest-living person included is Booker T. Washington, who was born in 1856 and died in 1915.

It was tempting to reach back to the days of Thomas Aquinas, Roger Bacon, and Leonardo Bruni, but we decided opening-up three centuries of additional writings complicated how we were trying to define the period. Nonetheless, those 13th and 14th century writers were deeply influential and foundational to the thinkers we reference.

Some scholars might take issue with our definition of the Enlightenment period, but we think it captures the era of ideas in the way that worked for the purposes of the book.

As for which geographies to focus on, this book features thinkers from Europe and America. We follow the progression of the Enlightenment as it moves through Europe and eventually to the newly-formed United States.

We recognize that the events of this time – creation of the printing press, advancement of science, 30-Years War, French Revolution, American Revolution, and the American debates on slavery and womens suffrage – all influenced both the thinking and the passages featured in this book. We hope that our analysis helps outline the context of current events and how the ideas were influenced by it.

Finally, the people who profiled in this book are by no means exhaustive of the important thinkers of the era. We made our decision based on which ideas were representative of the time, who we observed had influence, and admittedly which writers had produced enough work to study and analyze. We readily admit that some important thinkers are not included.

The product is an approachable text, which can either be used as a daily routine or could be easily read in a day, and hopefully re-read again and again. We hope it leads you to ask "why" more often in relation to your daily life, and spend each and every day just a little more intentionally.

365 Timeless Enlightenment Ideas

A Day-by-Day Dose of Reason

JANUARY 1

"The Beginning Is Always Today."

Mary Wollstonecraft Shelley

This is our January 1 quote for good reason – you have the ability to start fresh. A clean slate. "Tabula Rasa."

Wollstonecraft's words inspire us to embrace the present moment as an opportunity for new beginnings and growth. In a world that often fixates on past regrets or future anxieties, this quote reminds us that change and transformation are possible at any moment. It challenges us to let go of past failures or limitations and to seize the present moment as a chance to create the future we desire. It urges us to take action, pursue our aspirations, and embark on the journey of self-discovery and personal fulfillment.

JANUARY 2

"Do Not Go Where The Path May Lead, Go Instead Where There Is No Path And Leave A Trail."

Ralph Waldo Emerson

True to Emerson's strong individualism message that permeates so much of his writing, these words serve as a poignant reminder to embrace the spirit of innovation and creativity.

We can often find ourselves following the well-trodden paths laid out by others, following because because of pressure from our loved ones or colleagues, the pressure we place on ourselves, or simply because they can be the path of least resistance. True fulfillment and growth lie in venturing into uncharted territories, blazing our own trails, and carving out our unique paths in life. One with an individualist attitude will likely leave behind a legacy of courage, resilience, and authenticity, and living a meaningful and impactful life.

JANUARY 3

"Nothing Is Necessitated Whose Opposite Is Possible."

Gottfried Leibniz

Leibniz makes the deep point that if something can be one way, it could just as easily be the opposite. It is about freedom of choice and free will, that things are not inevitable or predetermined. Life can be a "choose your own ending" book.

The quote is in keeping with other philosophers of the time who were advocating skepticism of people and ideas that were too certain.

This idea resonates with our everyday experiences, reminding us that life is full of choices, chance, and possibilities, and that nothing is set in stone.

There is randomness everywhere in the world.

JANUARY 4

"Morning Without You Is A Dwindled Dawn."

Emily Dickinson

A poignant sentiment that reflects the profound impact of love and connection in our lives. Here, she seems to note that a morning without the people or person you love is a wasted moment.

The quote – from a letter written to a friend – challenges us to cherish the bonds that unite us. Regardless if it pertains to friendship or romance, recognize the value of love and companionship, realizing that true happiness arises from the warmth and intimacy of human connection.

Don't let too many mornings go by without being with those you treasure.

JANUARY 5

"Go Confidently In The Direction Of Your Dreams! Live The Life You've Imagined."

Henry David Thoreau

Reading Thoreau gives one a strong encouragement to live a life of self-determination, and this line is an excellent example. Thoreau's words inspire us to pursue our dreams with courage and conviction, unapologetically charting our own course in life.

It can be easy to fall into a life of conformity as it is often the path of less resistance, but this quote encourages us to trust in our aspirations, to embrace uncertainty, and to boldly pursue the life we envision for ourselves. True fulfillment comes from following our unique passions and living authentically, regardless of the obstacles or naysayers we may encounter along the way.

How will you spend today? Will you be taking a step – large or small – in the direction of your dreams?

JANUARY 6

"If Only We Wanted To Be Happy, It Would Be Easy; But We Want To Be Happier Than Other People, Which Is Difficult, Since We Think Them Happier Than They Are."

Charles de Montesquieu

Such a hard-hitting quote, in a day and age where so many people are benchmarking themselves against others – even those who they will never meet or know.

Montesquieu's observation shows that the tendency to compare ourselves with others is not new. Comparison and envy are as old as time.

We can work to create an authentic and fulfilling sense of well-being, independent of competing with others. Montesquieu might tell us to shift away from comparative success and toward a more grounded appreciation of life's simple joys. Determine your own standard for happiness, and then pursue it.

JANUARY 7

"Nature, To Be Commanded, Must Be Obeyed."

Francis Bacon

All you need to do is look at the effect of a wildfire, hurricane, or tsunami in the present day to realize that we don't tame nature, we simply learn to be part of it.

Bacon's insight into the relationship between humanity and nature underscores the importance of humility and respect in our interactions with the natural world.

By acknowledging the complexity and sheer power of nature, individuals and societies can cultivate sustainable and harmonious relationships with the environment. A healthy respect for the earth and natural world is a first step to enjoying it to the maximum.

JANUARY 8

"Man Is Born To Be Free, And Yet We Find Him Everywhere In Chains."

Jean-Jacques Rousseau

A profound line by Rousseau. It might seem like a quote about politics, but it is really about the human condition. One might argue that there is a dichotomy – we need to be part of society to enjoy its rewards, but by being part of it, we have to conform to some extent.

It is about the tension between personal liberty and societal norms and obligations.

Rousseau's repetition of the theme of human freedom underscores its fundamental importance to the human condition. We can recognize the inherent dignity and worth of every human being and strive for a society based on principles of equality and justice, where every individual has the opportunity to live a life of dignity and fulfillment, free from arbitrary constraints or limitations.

JANUARY 9

"Think For Yourself And Let Others Enjoy The Privilege Of Doing So Too."

Voltaire

Voltaire provides advice that is timeline. Be your own person, and don't try to control others or meddle in their thoughts. This sentiment is consistent with the personal liberty theme that was so prevalent during the Enlightenment.

Voltaire's advocacy for independent thinking, as expressed in this quote, aligns with his broader commitment to intellectual freedom and individual autonomy. In an era marked by censorship and intellectual repression, Voltaire championed the right of individuals to form their own opinions and engage in critical inquiry.

Try to approach others with respect for their opinions and approaches, but knowing that in the end you will decide what is right for you.

JANUARY 10

"All Our Knowledge Begins With The Senses, Proceeds Then To The Understanding, And Ends With Reason. There Is Nothing Higher Than Reason."

Immanuel Kant

This Kant line reinforces the belief of the Enlightenment thinkers, that reason was sacred and should be the driving force behind humans' actions.

Kant outlines the process of knowledge acquisition in this quote, starting from sensory experience, moving to conceptual understanding, and culminating in rational thought. He emphasizes the central role of reason in organizing and synthesizing our experiences and understanding.

This quote reflects Kant's epistemological views, or his views on how knowledge works, which emphasize the active role of the mind in constructing knowledge from sensory input.

JANUARY 11

"The great question which, in all ages, has disturbed mankind, and brought on them the greatest part of their mischiefs... has been, not whether be power in the world, nor whence it came, but who should have it."

John Locke

Locke's observation sheds light on the perennial struggle for power and its implications for human society. Today, as geopolitical tensions and social inequalities persist, Locke's insight remains relevant in understanding the dynamics of power and governance.

We can ask ourselves a few fundamental questions. How should people earn power? What should they need to do to keep it? Is the power at odds with the liberties of the masses?

Locke's timeless wisdom serves as a call to action, urging us to question the distribution of power and strive for a world where justice and liberty prevail.

JANUARY 12

"Energy and persistence conquer all things."

Benjamin Franklin

Franklin's succinct summary on the power of determination and perseverance reflects his belief in the indomitable human spirit, a mindset shaped by his own experiences of overcoming adversity.

Franklin understood the importance of resilience and tenacity in overcoming obstacles and achieving one's goals. His emphasis on the role of energy and persistence in conquering adversity resonates with individuals striving to overcome obstacles and achieve success in their own lives.

Perhaps the key message to all of us is this: When in doubt, keep pressing forward.

JANUARY 13

"Success is to be measured not so much by the position that one has reached in life as by the obstacles which he has overcome."

Booker T. Washington

Any parent proud of a child or family member proud of a loved one can probably relate to this Washington quote – that we are often more impressed by what they have overcome than anything else.

Washington emphasizes the importance of resilience and perseverance in achieving success. Setbacks and challenges are inevitable, but we can view success not merely in terms of status or achievements but in the ability to overcome obstacles and adversity along the way. Cultivate a mindset of determination and resilience, recognizing that true success is born out of the trials we overcome.

JANUARY 14

"Disturbances in society are never more fearful than when those who are stirring up the trouble can use the pretext of religion to mask their true designs."

Denis Diderot

Diderot notes that the most concerning disruptions in society arise when individuals exploit religion as a cover for their ulterior motives. When people manipulate religious beliefs to justify their actions, it obscures their true intentions and can lead to dangerous consequences.

Even among people who sincerely follow a religion, it is crucial to remain vigilant and discerning, separating genuine religious values from those who seek to exploit faith for personal gain or power.

Invoking religion, ideally, invites additional dialogue, discussion, and examination, not a "no further questions" mentality.

JANUARY 15

"If you are to be leaders, teachers, and guides among your people, you must have strength. No people can be fed, no people can be built up on flowers."

Alexander Crummell

Crummell's words highlight the indispensable quality of strength in leadership roles. People need their leaders to have a foundation and a moral compass.

He suggests that true leaders must possess inner fortitude and resilience to effectively support and guide others. The analogy of not being fed or built up on flowers underscores the idea that leadership requires substance and substance alone, emphasizing the importance of practicality and action over mere rhetoric or superficial gestures.

If you are in a leadership role, Crummell is reminding you of the challenges you will face and the necessity of strength to navigate them successfully.

JANUARY 16

"A woman indeed can't properly be said to choose, all that is allowed her, is to refuse or accept what is offered."

Mary Astell

Mary Astell's observation highlights the limited agency and autonomy afforded to women within patriarchal societies, such as hers around 1700.

By exposing the constraints imposed on women's choices and opportunities, Astell critiques the unequal power dynamics that govern gender relations – something she did frequently and compellingly.

The words reflect Astell's advocacy for women's rights and autonomy, underscoring her belief in the need for social and legal reforms to address the systemic inequalities faced by women.

JANUARY 17

"What you do speaks so loudly that I cannot hear what you say."

Ralph Waldo Emerson

A line that is reminiscent of the stoic philosophers and their focus on living a principled life. Emerson highlights the importance of integrity and action over mere words or rhetoric.

In all eras, people have struggled to deal with superficiality and empty promises, and this quote reminds us that our actions ultimately define who we are and how we are perceived by others. It urges us to align our words with our deeds, to live authentically, and to let our actions speak volumes about our character and values.

JANUARY 18

"Generally speaking, the errors in religion are dangerous; those in philosophy only ridiculous."

David Hume

A hard-hitting quote given the role religion has played in the shaping of society.

Mistakes within religious beliefs tend to carry significant consequences, often leading to harmful outcomes that alter the course of history. In contrast, errors made within philosophical reasoning are typically viewed as harmless or amusing.

This distinction underscores the potential impact of misinformation or misguided beliefs within religious contexts. The passion which believers of various religions might have for their beliefs can result in serious conflict, even war.

JANUARY 19

"Thought means life, since those who do not think do not live in any high or real sense. Thinking makes the man."

Amos Alcott

A quote that resembles those of Alcott's friends, Emerson and Thoreau.

Alcott's reflection on the power of thought underscores the transformative impact of intellectual engagement and curiosity. It reminds us that true living involves more than mere existence; it requires curiosity, and active engagement with ideas and concepts that challenge and enrich our understanding of the world.

Cultivate a habit of critical thinking and reflection, recognizing that our thoughts shape our perceptions, beliefs, and ultimately, our lives.

JANUARY 20

"It is unworthy of excellent men to lose hours like slaves in the labour of calculation which could safely be relegated to anyone else if machines were used."

Gottfried Leibniz

Some context: Leibniz wrote this in a letter to a group of astronomers, outlining the value of a hand-cranking calculating machine he had built.

Leibniz's reflection underscores the transformative potential of technology in liberating human intellect from mundane tasks and fostering intellectual creativity.

Especially in today's digital era, where automation and artificial intelligence continue to revolutionize various industries, Leibniz's insight serves as a reminder of the importance of leveraging technology to augment human capabilities. This quote might help us deal with the rapid advancements in artificial intelligence that we are seeing – and perhaps a bit worried about – today.

JANUARY 21

"Insults are the arguments employed by those who are in the wrong."

Jean-Jacques Rousseau

Such an insightful quote, written in the concise way that Rousseau was so effective at.

Those who can debate their case on the merits and facts of their position do so. Those who can't – well, they often resort to personal attacks and insults. Perhaps it is the only way for them to look strong, in their minds.

We see this often today, in our politics, social media, and other venues. Even though Rousseau's words were written nearly 300 years ago, they might be even more relevant today.

JANUARY 22

"Character is power."

Booker T. Washington

Washington emphasizes the transformative power of moral integrity and ethical conduct, and distills a profound truth about the nature of influence and efficacy. In just three words, he encapsulates the essence of personal agency, suggesting that one's character is not only a reflection of their inner values but also a source of formidable strength in navigating life's challenges.

In our contemporary culture often preoccupied with external markers of success and influence, Washington's assertion serves as a timely reminder of the enduring significance of moral character. Perhaps we should ask ourselves, "If everyone saw character as the most powerful trait, how would we change? How would the world change?"

JANUARY 23

"Happiest are the people who give most happiness to others."

Denis Diderot

As children, we learned that "it is better to give than to receive." Diderot's assertion underscores the profound joy that arises from altruism and benevolence.

By emphasizing the importance of bringing happiness to others, Diderot notes that the giver will become happy themselves. This quote reflects Diderot's belief in the intrinsic value of compassion and empathy, highlighting the transformative power of selflessness in fostering genuine happiness and well-being for both individuals and communities.

Go out in the world, and do something good for someone. You both will benefit.

JANUARY 24

"Never leave that till tomorrow which you can do today."

Benjamin Franklin

Franklin's pithy and concise communication style created a treasure trove of quotes, and this is one you have likely seen before.

Franklin's admonition against procrastination reflects his belief in the importance of diligence and prompt action in achieving success, a mindset shaped by the challenges and opportunities of his time.

Franklin's words still serve as a reminder of the importance of seizing the moment and making the most of one's time and talents, and the timeless wisdom of taking initiative and tackling tasks promptly and decisively.

JANUARY 25

"The more clearly you understand yourself and your emotions, the more you become a lover of what is."

Baruch Spinoza

An insightful quote by Spinoza, saying that when you really know yourself well, including your feelings and emotions, you're more likely to appreciate and embrace the world around you. Spinoza suggests that understanding yourself deeply helps you develop a love for things as they are, rather than wishing for them to be different.

This quote speaks to the importance of self-awareness in understanding the actions and motivations of the people we interact with. It suggests that when individuals truly understand themselves, they are better equipped to navigate their own lives and relationships, and perhaps even influence the world around them in a positive way.

JANUARY 26

"Very early, I knew that the only object in life was to grow."

Margaret Fuller

For a shift in perspective, simply ask yourself "Will I grow today?"

Fuller's reflection on personal growth underscores the importance of continuous learning and self-improvement in the pursuit of fulfillment and purpose. With busy, predefined, schedules, it can be hard to prioritize inner growth and development. Recognize that true fulfillment comes not from reaching a destination but from the journey of growth and self-realization.

By reading this book, you have taken one small step toward daily growth.

JANUARY 27

"To be thrown upon one's own resources is to be cast into the very lap of fortune; for our faculties then undergo a development and display an energy of which they were previously unsusceptible."

Benjamin Franklin

"To make your own way" has long been viewed with respect, and Franklin's reflection on self-reliance underscores the transformative power of adversity in unlocking human potential and resilience.

So many dream of a life where our needs are magically met through a stroke of good luck. Such a life, though, can shield us from challenges that make us better, and this quote reminds us to embrace adversity as an opportunity for growth and self-discovery. It urges us to tap into our inner resources and ingenuity, recognizing that adversity has the power to catalyze personal growth and unleash hidden talents and capabilities.

JANUARY 28

"We are either progressing or retrograding all the while; there is no such thing as remaining stationary in this life."

James Freeman Clarke

What an observation on the importance of an upward trajectory.

Clarke's reflection on personal growth underscores the dynamic nature of human experience and the inevitability of change. The quote drives home that nothing is static, and that if you are not growing, then you are likely declining. Embrace change as a natural and necessary part of life and adopt a mindset of continuous improvement and self-reflection, recognizing that stagnation leads to decline while growth leads to fulfillment and vitality.

JANUARY 29

"A true teacher defends his students against his own personal influences."

Amos Alcott

Alcott, the student of educational theory and practice, realized that the teacher's own bias can get in the way of learning.

Alcott's reflection on teaching underscores the importance of fostering independent thinking and autonomy in education. It reinforces the need to empower students to think critically and form their own judgments.

If you find yourself as the teacher, are your own biases influencing what you teach? Or are you giving the student the best information for them to grow and build their own knowledge?

JANUARY 30

"I have made a ceaseless effort not to ridicule, not to bewail, not to scorn human actions, but to understand them."

Baruch Spinoza

Spinoza's commitment to understanding human behavior offers a valuable lesson in empathy and compassion.

So often, judgment and condemnation are what gets the headline or the engagement. Spinoza's wisdom reminds us of the importance of seeking to understand rather than to judge or criticize.

As with so many Enlightenment ideas, Spinoza is suggesting a mindset of curiosity and empathy, recognizing that every action is shaped by a complex interplay of factors. By approaching others with understanding and compassion, we foster harmony and a more intelligent understanding of what is going on around us.

JANUARY 31

"No one should part with their individuality and become that of another."

William Ellery Channing

IF THE AMERICAN Renaissance celebrated individualism and free will, Channing's quote is a good encapsulation of it. It underscores the importance of preserving and honoring our own unique identities and perspectives in the face of external pressures and influences.

If Channing were around today, perhaps he would tell us to remain true to our own values, beliefs, and aspirations, especially in light of the temptation to conform to societal expectations driven by influencers, social media, and constant comparison with others.

FEBRUARY 1

"Why should we build our happiness on the opinions of others, when we can find it in our own hearts?"

Jean-Jacques Rousseau

Such an important lesson today, centuries after Rousseau wrote it, given how much of current society's happiness tends to come from external validation.

Rousseau's inquiry challenges the societal norms that often dictate our pursuit of happiness based on the feedback we receive from others. In today's era of social media and constant comparison, Rousseau's wisdom reminds us of the importance of introspection and self-awareness in cultivating genuine fulfillment from within.

Only you can judge if you are happy, accomplished, or if you had a good day. Don't rely too much on validation from others.

FEBRUARY 2

"The highest perfection of intellectual nature lies in a careful and constant pursuit of true and solid happiness."

John Locke

You can see many of the American Transcendentalist thinkers in this Locke quote from nearly 200 years before their time.

Locke"s insight underscores the importance of aligning intellectual pursuits with the quest for genuine fulfillment and contentment. Locke suggests that we should prioritize the pursuit of happiness as the ultimate aim of intellectual endeavor. Learning and self discovery will drive contentment and happiness.

FEBRUARY 3

"As a single footstep will not make a path on the earth, so a single thought will not make a pathway in the mind. To make a deep physical path, we walk again and again. To make a deep mental path, we must think over and over the kind of thoughts we wish to dominate our lives."

Henry David Thoreau

Thoreau is not often labeled as a personal productivity guru, but this passage provides a template for changing one's mindset and attitude. Thoreau's analogy underscores the importance of repetition and consistency in shaping our mindset. It is in line with the popular genre of habit books today.

Thoreau reminds us that meaningful change and growth require sustained effort and commitment, and that up-leveling your mindset require lots of reinforcement. By walking the path of intentional living with purpose, we pave the way for a life of fulfillment and significance.

FEBRUARY 4

"Keep your face always toward the sunshine - and shadows will fall behind you."

Walt Whitman

Whitman's uplifting line underscores the transformative power of optimism and positive thinking in navigating life's challenges.

By keeping your attention attracted to what is in front of you, what is interesting and captivating, you can ignore the negativity of the world around you. This quote challenges us to focus on the bright possibilities and opportunities that lie ahead and to cultivate a mindset of resilience and hope.

FEBRUARY 5

"Beauty is no quality in things themselves: It exists merely in the mind which contemplates them."

David Hume

How many times have you heard "beauty is in the eye of the beholder"? Hume apparently would have agreed.

This line underscores the subjectivity of aesthetic experience. The fact is that beauty standards of the day often dictate our perceptions. It is possible that beauty is not an inherent quality of objects, but rather a subjective interpretation shaped by individual perspective and perception.

Approach everything you encounter with a wide-open mind. You just might find more beautiful things and experiences that way.

FEBRUARY 6

"The mass of men lead lives of quiet desperation."

Henry David Thoreau

Thoreau's writing can sometimes be critical and melancholy, and this line is no exception. His observation serves as a poignant reminder of the pervasive sense of dissatisfaction and disillusionment that can afflict people many of whom quietly accept it.

It seems that Thoreau is encouraging today's reader to reflect on the true sources of happiness and meaning in our lives. The quote challenges us to break free from the chains of conformity and consumerism, to seek authenticity and purpose, and to live deliberately with intention and passion. In other words, if you don't like your life, change something.

FEBRUARY 7

"We build too many walls and not enough bridges."

Sir Isaac Newton

This metaphor has been used often since the days of Newton, especially in political and policy talks and writings.

Newton's observation on the human tendency to erect barriers rather than foster connections speaks to the need for greater empathy and understanding in society. Newton's words inspire us to strive for unity and solidarity, recognizing that it is through collaboration and empathy that we can overcome the challenges facing our world today.

As a disclaimer, this quote is sometimes attributed to American Minister Joseph Fort Newton, but our research traces it back to Sir Isaac Newton.

FEBRUARY 8

"People who know little are usually great talkers, while men who know much say little."

Jean-Jacques Rousseau

Rousseau's observation about the correlation between knowledge and speech highlights the importance of humility and self-awareness in communication. How often have we heard someone work to dominate our attention only to realize that they are thin on either knowledge or reason?

In today's age of information overload and constant discourse, Rousseau's wisdom serves as a reminder to value substance over verbosity.

This goes not only for people who you are listening to; you can use it to improve yourself. Be sure you are speaking from a place of reason, knowledge, and fact. Keep your communications tight and informative, try not to be one who simply talks just to talk.

FEBRUARY 9

"Do anything, but let it produce joy."

Walt Whitman

Whitman's writing simplicity is impressive. It is no surprise that his poetry is what he is best-remembered for.

This reflection emphasizes the importance of finding joy and fulfillment in your life's pursuits. Your time on earth is limited, so engage in activities and pursuits that bring you joy and fulfillment.

True success is in doing something that brings joy. Only you can decide what that is.

FEBRUARY 10

"It is not enough to have a good mind; the main thing is to use it well."

René Descartes

It has been noted that smart people with the wrong intentions become the most dangerous people.

While Descartes might be referring to sinister people in this passage, he might also be referring to people who simply don't apply themselves to higher ideals of constructive activity.

The quote comes from Descartes' seminal work, *Discourse on the Method*, which focuses on the role of skepticism in questioning things and arriving at truth. To that end, Descartes seems to be suggesting that a well-trained mind applied in the right direction can help us arrive at greater truths.

FEBRUARY 11

"The office of government is not to confer happiness, but to give men the opportunity to work out happiness for themselves."

William Ellery Channing

A line that is true to the strong self-reliance thread of the American Enlightenment movement.

Channing's reflection on the role of government underscores the importance of freedom and autonomy in fostering individual fulfillment and well-being. The exercise of personal agency and responsibility is not only good for society, but Channing suggests it is better for the individual, too. The quote urges us to cultivate a society that values individual liberty and opportunity, empowering citizens to pursue their own paths to happiness and fulfillment.

FEBRUARY 12

"A kindergarten! what is that?' 'A garden whose plants are human."

Elizabeth Peabody

Peabody, one of the earliest proponents (at least on record) for early childhood education, was always viewing the classroom as a place where children could flourish.

Here, Peabody notes, in a letter to a parent who is downplaying the role of kindergarten, how wondrous a kindergarten classroom is. Likening it to a garden, she makes one envision seeds that simply need water and care, and they will grow and develop.

If you have children in your life, treat them all like a seed that wants to grow – a precious and desirable being that is thirsty for your guidance and teaching.

FEBRUARY 13

"The greatest thing in this world is not so much where we stand as in what direction we are moving."

Oliver Wendell Holmes

Holmes was known for an optimism and energy, and a humility that was often unexpected for a legal mind of such stature. Despite his authoritative position, he always knew that there was more he would learn and he did not have everything mastered.

Perhaps this quote comes from that humility, the idea that regardless of where you are today, it is what you intend to do tomorrow and the next day that will be the measure of your life.

Regardless of where you find yourself, you can always take steps in the direction you intend.

FEBRUARY 14

"Prejudices are what fools use for reason."

Voltaire

Sometimes the intellectually lazy route is to fall back on the beliefs you have always had, beliefs that might exist because of tradition or simply because they have never been examined.

Voltaire's critique of prejudice underscores the dangers of narrow-mindedness and bigotry in human affairs. It encourages us to question our own biases and assumptions and to cultivate empathy and understanding for others, both in who they are as well as their point of view.

FEBRUARY 15

"I am suffocated and lost when I have not the bright feeling of progression."

Margaret Fuller

Fuller's reflection on the importance of progression underscores the human desire for growth and advancement. Stagnation can lead to feelings of despair and dissatisfaction, and can create a self-perpetuating cycle of sameness. This quote challenges us to embrace change and evolution as essential aspects of life. It urges us to set goals and aspirations that inspire us to grow and develop, both personally and professionally. It reminds us that the pursuit of progress is not just a means to an end but a source of vitality, meaning, and fulfillment in itself.

FEBRUARY 16

"Do I contradict myself? Very well then I contradict myself,"

Walt Whitman

Such a great lesson, especially perhaps for political observers. Don't be dug-in, don't be inflexible. Intake new information, examine your views, and constantly strive to make your positions even more sound, even if it means you will admit being wrong before.

Whitman's acknowledgment and acceptance of contradiction reflect a nuanced understanding of complexity and evolution. The need to pivot and adapt in the face of changing circumstances is really an affirmation of growth and self-discovery. Embrace change and embrace contradictions as natural parts of personal and creative development.

FEBRUARY 17

"...that every individual spontaneously tries to find the place and the trade in which he can best increase National gain, if laws do not prevent him from doing so."

Anders Chydenius

Here, Chydenius, the part-time trade negotiator, articulates the innate drive of individuals to contribute to the collective welfare of their nation through productive endeavors.

He contends that, given the opportunity, individuals will naturally seek out roles that align with their abilities and interests, thereby enhancing national prosperity. However, he warns against restricting this freedom through law, instead favoring free trade and commerce.

Chydenius lived in Sweden at about the same time that Adam Smith lived in Scotland. Some of their work is very reminiscent of each other's, such as this passage.

FEBRUARY 18

"Happiness is like a butterfly: the more you chase it, the more it will elude you, but if you turn your attention to other things, it will come and sit softly on your shoulder."

Henry David Thoreau

Thoreau seems to be saying to us, "Don't force it."

He also seems to be noting the paradoxical nature of happiness – and the importance of pursuing it indirectly. Approaching the world with an attitude of acceptance and gratitude might be the best way to find ourselves in a happy state.

It has been said that pursuing contentment is more realistic than pursuing happiness. Perhaps Thoreau is saying that one doesn't pursue happiness, but instead they create a state where it will find them.

FEBRUARY 19

"Words - so innocent and powerless as they are, as standing in a dictionary, how potent for good and evil they become in the hands of one who knows how to combine them."

Nathaniel Hawthorne

Hawthorne underscores the art behind a turn-of-phrase. Simple words can be innocuous in their isolated form within a dictionary, yet capable of immense influence when deftly wielded by a skilled communicator.

Hawthorne highlights the dual potential of words to inspire enlightenment or sow discord, depending on the intentions of the speaker or writer. He invites us to consider the balance between expression and consequence—a timeless theme that continues to resonate in our increasingly interconnected world.

You can use words for profound, good things, or for negative or petty ends. Which will you choose?

FEBRUARY 20

"If you could blow the brain up to the size of a mill and walk about inside, you would not find consciousness."

Gottfried Leibniz

Leibniz's metaphorical statement challenges conventional notions of consciousness and invites contemplation on the elusive nature of subjective experience. Consciousness is not something you attain just by filling your brain with ideas and knowledge.

Leibniz offers a perspective that transcends mere physicality. Rather than attempting to conquer it, appreciate the nuanced and enigmatic nature of consciousness, recognizing its ineffable qualities and resisting reductionist explanations.

It is OK for there to be some mystery in this world.

FEBRUARY 21

"The tyranny of a prince in an oligarchy is not so dangerous to the public welfare as the apathy of a citizen in a democracy."

Montesquieu

Montesquieu's comparison highlights the paradoxical nature of democracy, where the greatest threat to freedom is often indifference and complacency.

Montesquieu was a persistent advocate for shifting power to the people, but in this line, he notes that with that power shift comes an important responsibility. If power is shifted to people who don't care, perhaps the government would be better off in the old oligarch ways.

Civic engagement tends to wane, and this line serves as an important reminder that there is real danger in citizens not being interested in their democratic government.

FEBRUARY 22

"There is frequently more to be learned from the unexpected questions of a child than the discourses of men."

John Locke

How often have you gotten a question from a child that was rooted in such straightforward logic that it was difficult to answer?

Locke's observation on the insightful nature of children's questions highlights the importance of curiosity and open-mindedness in intellectual exploration. Children are not saddled with decades or centuries of nuance and context, or with a resignation that "that is how we've always done it."

Locke's wisdom encourages us to approach intellectual inquiry with humility and a willingness to learn from unexpected sources, fostering a culture of lifelong learning and discovery. Bring a fresh set of eyes to the problems you are trying to solve.

FEBRUARY 23

"You may delay, but time will not."

Benjamin Franklin

Franklin's pithy observation on the inexorable passage of time reflects his keen awareness of the fleeting nature of life and the importance of seizing the moment.

His emphasis on the irreversibility of time resonates with modern readers, underscoring the importance of living with intention and purpose, and making the most of the time we have.

It is a bad feeling to realize that time has passed and you have not accomplished what you should have. Work to be the person who makes the most of this day and every day.

FEBRUARY 24

"Time flies over us, but leaves its shadow behind."

Nathaniel Hawthorne

Two time quotes in a row. The passage of time has been contemplated as long as humans have had thought. Here, Hawthorne underscores the fleeting nature of life and the enduring impact of our experiences and memories.

Time seems to accelerate with each passing year, but as it passes the world is not unchanged. It leaves its mark, with us left to try to catch-up and make sense of how quickly it is moving.

Perhaps the best thing you can do, given the inevitable march of the clock, is to seize every day and enjoy what it brings you.

FEBRUARY 25

"To know what people really think, pay attention to what they do, rather than what they say."

René Descartes

Many Enlightenment Era passages refer to some variation of the adage "actions speak louder than words," and in this Descartes line we see the same sentiment. It is a theme that the seekers of reason kept coming back to, perhaps because they were so disillusioned by dogma and instructions coming from leaders who they distrusted.

The line is instructive, both in how we interact with others but how we carry ourselves.

Can you take someone at their word? Have their actions proven that they are trustworthy, and do they align with what they say?

At the same time, are you someone who, if others are watching your actions, would be viewed as admirable? It is a good test.

FEBRUARY 26

"Silence is the sleep that nourishes wisdom."

Francis Bacon

Much has been written in recent years about the value of a quiet, calm mind. Perhaps Bacon was ahead of his time with this line.

Bacon notes that introspection and contemplation are key elements to the pursuit of wisdom. People who make time for solitude and reflection are better equipped to cultivate clarity of thought and insight.

Moments of silence are opportunities for self-discovery, cerebral breakthroughs, and renewal. It is a reminder for us that idle time spent thinking is not lazy, but rather intellectually quite productive, and should be prioritized.

FEBRUARY 27

"The purpose of life is not to be happy. It is to be useful, to be honorable, to be compassionate, to have it make some difference that you have lived and lived well."

Ralph Waldo Emerson

The transcendentalists spent lots of effort trying to define the potential of the individual and their true purpose, and Emerson challenges conventional notions of happiness and success, which were exacerbated by the Gilded Age toward the end of his life, proposing a more profound and meaningful purpose for life.

The pursuit of happiness and personal gratification is often still glorified, but this quote invites us to shift our focus towards serving others, acting with integrity, and leaving a positive impact on the world. True fulfillment comes not from self-serving pursuits but from living a life of purpose, virtue, and contribution to the greater good.

FEBRUARY 28

"Life is made up of marble and mud."

Nathaniel Hawthorne

Hawthorne's metaphor captures the dualities and contradictions inherent in the human experience, marble being the output – or the possessions – and mud being the hard work involved along the way.

In a world where moments of triumph and beauty are often tempered by periods of struggle and adversity, this quote challenges us to embrace the full spectrum of life's experiences. It urges us to navigate the highs and lows with resilience and grace, recognizing that it is through the contrast of light and shadow, joy and sorrow, that the richness and complexity of life are revealed.

"The journey is the reward" might be another way to say this.

MARCH 1

"It is a curious subject of observation and inquiry, whether hatred and love be not the same thing at bottom."

Nathaniel Hawthorne

Consider this intriguing question: at their core, are hatred and love not two sides of the same coin? Both emotions stem from a deep intensity of feeling and a profound connection to the subject of our emotions.

The answer might lie in our ability to channel these powerful energies towards positivity and compassion. By understanding the interconnectedness of these emotions, we can harness the transformative power of love to overcome hatred and division, fostering empathy, understanding, and unity in our communities and beyond.

But beware - it is a slippery slope. The same passion that creates love could create hatred if channeled incorrectly.

MARCH 2

"Only passions, great passions, can elevate the soul to great things."

Denis Diderot

Do you love what you are working on?

Diderot suggests that only if we are passionate about what we are doing, can we experience, create, or achieve great things. His insight underscores the transformative power of passion in driving human endeavor and achievement.

We all know we should pursue our dreams with vigor and determination and channel our energy and enthusiasm into meaningful pursuits. The hard part can be transforming your life to focus on those pursuits, but it is possible.

MARCH 3

"To prejudge other men's notions before we have looked into them is not to show their darkness but to put out our own eyes."

John Locke

The old stoics were always careful to beware that they might be the ones who were wrong, and Locke carries that same sentiment in this line.

Locke's admonition against prejudging others' ideas serves as a direct reminder of the importance of intellectual humility and open-mindedness in fostering meaningful dialogue and understanding.

Perhaps this is even more true today than when Locke wrote it, with our narrow news sources and echo chambers. Locke's insight offers a timely call to embrace intellectual curiosity and empathy, and to remember that true enlightenment comes from embracing the richness and diversity of human thought.

MARCH 4

"I can calculate the motion of heavenly bodies, but not the madness of people."

Sir Isaac Newton

This humorous line from Newton distills the fact that things – however complicated – are often easier to understand than people.

Newton's observation on the unpredictability of human behavior highlights the limitations of scientific inquiry in understanding the complexities of the human psyche. Despite his mastery of the laws of physics and mathematics, Newton acknowledges he struggles with understanding humans and societies.

As you go about your endeavors, keep in mind that the moments requiring the most skill and effort will likely be those where you are dealing with other people.

MARCH 5

"Common sense is not so common."

Voltaire

Voltaire notes the rarity of clear, practical thinking in the world.

As we navigate challenges and opportunities, it's essential to cultivate and rely on this uncommon trait to cut through the noise and focus on what truly matters.

One could argue that common sense is a blend of information intake and experience-based intuition, combining simplicity, clarity, and practicality in both business and life. Rationality and pragmatism are at its heart.

MARCH 6

"There is only one passion, the passion for happiness."

Denis Diderot

Diderot often wrote about the link between passion and happiness. He believed the two needed to co-exist for either to be present.

His insight underscores the transformative power of passion in driving human endeavor and achievement. Moreover, he notes that passion can be a means to an end, but that end is always and should be happiness.

Bringing energy and enthusiasm to our pursuits, and being truly enthralled by our life's work, is the way to achieve fulfillment and happiness.

MARCH 7

"It is too difficult to think nobly when one thinks only of earning a living."

Jean-Jacques Rousseau

In this insightful quote by Rousseau, he suggests that focusing solely on making a living can hinder our ability to think and act with nobility. When our primary concern is earning money to survive, we lose sight of higher ideals and values. Rousseau is pointing out the challenge of maintaining moral integrity and pursuing noble goals in a society where financial concerns often take precedence.

Rousseau encourages us to consider how our priorities and actions are influenced by economic pressures, and reminds us of the importance of aspiring to nobility of thought and action, even in the face of practical challenges.

Is your need for a living causing you to live in a less-principled way?

MARCH 8

"A thing is not proved just because no one has ever questioned it."

Denis Diderot

Diderot was a skeptic, and this quote embodies that world view.

Simply because something has not been questioned does not make it inherently true or valid. True innovation and progress come from challenging the status quo and questioning assumptions. It's through this critical examination that we uncover new insights and possibilities, driving meaningful change and advancement.

Ask "why?" more often, about more things you encounter. There is a good chance that nobody else ever has.

MARCH 9

"The life of man is of no greater importance to the universe than that of an oyster."

David Hume

Hume's reflection on the insignificance of human existence in the grand scheme of the universe underscores the humility and perspective required for true wisdom.

Human nature causes egocentrism and self-importance to often cloud our judgment, and this quote challenges us to recognize the fleeting nature of human life and the vastness of the cosmos.

Before you begin to take yourself too seriously, just remember that your place in the world is quite tiny and insignificant. Your meaning and satisfaction need to come from within.

MARCH 10

"The inner self is as distinct from the outer self as heaven is from earth."

Emmanuel Swedenborg

We are all multi-dimensional, and who the person is on the outside is so very different from who the person is on the inside.

Swedenborg's metaphorical comparison challenges us to recognize the duality of our existence and the interconnectedness of our inner and outer worlds, and cultivate integrity and congruence in our actions and behaviors.

It is also an encouraging idea, in a way, that even if the physical body is scarred, weakening, or aging, the inner mind and soul can still be sharp, vibrant, and growing.

MARCH 11

"There are three principal means of acquiring knowledge: observation of nature, reflection, and experimentation. Observation collects facts; reflection combines them; experimentation verifies the result of that combination."

Denis Diderot

A fun mental framework from Diderot that represents the time's advancement of the scientific method. Diderot highlights the empirical inquiry and rational analysis in the pursuit of knowledge.

The passage could be taken as a "back to the basics" lesson today, as such an influx of information, data, and analytics sometimes feels like it skips a step or two.

Observe, reflect, and verify. A good way to solve problems and learn new things.

MARCH 12

"I do not wish women to have power over men; but over themselves."

Mary Wollstonecraft Shelley

Wollstonecraft provides some useful perspective to her reader, reminding them what she is really fighting for. This was at a time when many women felt unempowered.

Wollstonecraft's words emphasize the importance of women's autonomy and self-determination. In a patriarchal society that often denies women agency and control over their own lives, this quote advocates for women's empowerment and liberation from oppressive social norms and expectations. It challenges us to recognize women as individuals with their own desires, ambitions, and rights, deserving of respect, equality, and freedom.

MARCH 13

"Useless laws weaken the necessary laws."

Montesquieu

Such a simple line, but at the same time such a true and important one.

Montesquieu's observation highlights the danger of legislative overreach and bureaucratic inefficiency. We must prioritize clarity and effectiveness in governance, and streamline legal frameworks and eliminate unnecessary regulations, making laws that are clear, concise, and enforceable.

The concept can apply to our work, organizations, or even our family lives. When it comes to rules, get rid of the noise. That will leave a clearer focus on the important principles.

MARCH 14

"Conquer yourself rather than the world."

René Descartes

In this concise yet profound statement, Descartes emphasizes the importance of self-mastery and inner growth over external conquest.

He suggests that true fulfillment and success lie not in dominating others or achieving material ambitions, but in mastering our own thoughts, emotions, and desires. The journey of self-discovery and self-improvement is the most meaningful and transformative endeavor one can undertake. Rather than seeking validation or power from external sources, Descartes invites us to look inward first.

For those who are particularly competitive, this quote might be instructive. Focus more on improving yourself, and pursuing personal excellence, and less on keeping score against others.

MARCH 15

"The greatness of peoples springs from their ability to grasp the grand conceptions of being. It is the absorption of a people, of a nation, of a rare, in large majestic and abiding things which lifts them up to the skies."

Alexander Crummell

Crummell's reflection on greatness underscores the transformative power of visionary thinking and lofty aspirations. He suggests that the true essence of greatness lies in a society's capacity to embrace profound ideals and pursue noble endeavors that transcend individual interests.

Try to rise above the day to day, above the mundane to-do list that might be dictating your day. Inject something profound into your life.

MARCH 16

**"A nation which thinks that it is belief in God
and not good law which makes people honest
does not seem to me very advanced."**

Denis Diderot

The Enlightenment was an era of being skeptical of organized religion, although many of the thinkers were highly-spiritual themselves.

Diderot's critique of the notion that religious belief alone determines morality challenges prevailing attitudes towards the role of religion in society. He suggests that true progress lies in the development of rational laws and ethical principles rather than reliance on supernatural doctrines.

This quote reflects Diderot's commitment to secularism being the driving force of rules, and his advocacy for the separation of church and state.

MARCH 17

"The perfect is the enemy of the good."

Voltaire

A Voltaire line that has made its way into the lexicon of modern-day business and leadership. Voltaire's aphorism highlights the pitfalls of perfectionism and idealism in human endeavors. The pursuit of perfection often leads to paralysis or dissatisfaction, creating an urge to simply do nothing.

Instead of waiting on perfection, simply take a step in the direction of good. If you constantly do, through continuous refinement, your ideas, actions, and results will be elevated beyond those waiting for the perfect situation.

MARCH 18

"We are not rich by what we possess but by what we can do without."

Immanuel Kant

Kant touches upon the idea of true wealth not being measured by material possessions, but by our ability to live without relying solely on them. This sentiment reflects Kant's emphasis on inner worth and personal fulfillment rather than external wealth.

Kant suggests that true richness comes from our capacity for self-sufficiency and contentment with what we have, aligning with Kant's broader philosophical views on human dignity and autonomy.

If you are pursuing wealth or possessions, consider doing a reset. Freedom comes from being happy with less, and being able to "Simplify" in the words of Thoreau.

MARCH 19

"Skepticism is the first step on the road to philosophy."

Denis Diderot

Embracing skepticism is the essential starting point for anyone seeking deeper understanding and innovation.

Diderot aptly points out that skepticism is the catalyst that propels us to question assumptions, challenge conventions, and ultimately pave the way for transformative ideas and breakthroughs.

Skepticism need not be negative, but In cultivating a mindset of critical thinking, we open ourselves to the possibilities of true enlightenment and progress.

MARCH 20

"The means of obtaining as much variety as possible, but with the greatest possible order...is the means of obtaining as much perfection as possible."

Gottfried Leibniz

A line that evokes The Law of Large Numbers, in a way.

Leibniz's proposition on variety and order underscores the importance of balance and harmony in achieving excellence. It offers a guiding principle for navigating the intricacies of life.

By embracing variety, diversity, and creativity within a framework of organization and discipline, individuals can maximize their potential for success and fulfillment. Leibniz's wisdom encourages us to seek perfection not through rigid uniformity, but through the dynamic interplay of variety and order in our endeavors.

MARCH 21

"A wise man proportions his belief to the evidence."

David Hume

This quote is true to form for Hume, who always encouraged us to insist on credible proof and reasoning when examining information. In this line, he takes it a step further and suggests that the less abundant the proof, the less we should adopt the belief.

Hume's principle of epistemic humility underscores the importance of intellectual honesty and skepticism in the pursuit of knowledge and understanding.

We will always encounter dogmatism and people who are overly-certain about things. Hume suggests that we keep our guard up, and avoid falling for firm conclusions based on limited evidence, data, or proof.

MARCH 22

"A judge is required to complete a perfect syllogism in which the major premise must be the general law; the action that conforms or does not conform to the law; and the conclusion, acquittal or punishment. If the judge... desired to frame even a single additional syllogism, the door would thereby be opened to uncertainty."

Cesare Beccaria

Beccaria highlights the importance of a judge adhering strictly to the law when making decisions. Any deviation from applying the specific laws in question to the specific details of the case introduces uncertainty and subjectivity into the judicial system.

This quote underscores the significance of consistency and adherence to legal principles in ensuring justice. Straying from consistency can allow things like subjectivity, personal feeling, or even corruption to enter the picture, which undermines justice.

MARCH 23

"I would rather be a man of paradoxes than a man of prejudices."

Jean-Jacques Rousseau

Rousseau's preference for paradoxes over prejudices speaks to the value of critical thinking and intellectual curiosity in navigating complex moral and philosophical questions. He seems to be telling us that it is OK to accept nuance in our ideas; that some degree of subtlety is preferable to the more simplistic beliefs that can result in unwarranted biases.

It is possible Rousseau drew this belief from his own life experience. His writing of *Social Contract* caused some scandals and no doubt gave him thick skin.

Rousseau's wisdom serves as a reminder to embrace nuance and open-mindedness in our approach to understanding the world. When you drill into them, few questions can be reduced to a simple either/or answer.

MARCH 24

"What worries you masters you."

John Locke

In the succinct yet profound utterance of John Locke, we encounter a distilled truth that resonates with the echoes of timeless wisdom. Locke's concise assertion serves as a penetrating inquiry into the intricate workings of the human psyche and the dynamics of power within the individual.

Evoking a palpable sense of agency and vulnerability, Locke invites us to confront the intimate interplay between our anxieties and our capacity for self-mastery. Within this terse proclamation lies a profound reflection on the fundamental relationship between the human condition and the forces that shape it.

MARCH 25

"Kindness is an inner desire that makes us want to do good things even if we do not get anything in return. It is the joy of our life to do them. When we do good things from this inner desire, there is kindness in everything we think, say, want, and do."

Emmanuel Swedenborg

A common theme from Swedenborg is to find joy in giving and being selfless. Here, his insight into the nature of kindness challenges us to cultivate a genuine spirit of altruism and benevolence in our daily lives.

One could argue that today's world is excessively about personal gain, and this quote serves as a reminder of the intrinsic value of acts of kindness and generosity.

Kindness is not merely a gesture, but a way of being—a reflection of the goodness that resides within us and the potential we have to make a positive difference in the world.

MARCH 26

"Experience without theory is blind, but theory without experience is mere intellectual play."

Immanuel Kant

Kant emphasizes the importance of both theory and experience in this quote. He suggests that theory, or abstract ideas, needs to be grounded in real-world experience to be meaningful and useful. Similarly, experience without a theoretical framework to make sense of it can lack direction and understanding.

A balance of grounding your actions with a framework or reasoning is important, but so is taking action and not simply having every idea be a purely academic exercise.

This quote reflects Kant's holistic approach to knowledge, which combines rational thought with empirical observation.

MARCH 27

"Resist much, obey little."

Walt Whitman

Whitman's directive encapsulates the spirit of nonconformity and individualism. It is hard not to see it as a call to challenge the status quo and think independently.

In modern day, we could view this as a license to push for innovation through rebellion against established norms, and emphasize the importance of questioning authority and embracing a mindset that prioritizes creativity and self-expression over blind adherence to rules or conventions.

Resisting might mean being defiant, or it can simply mean being skeptical and asking "why?" Either way, you are forcing society to examine itself.

MARCH 28

"I have not been able to discover the cause of those properties of gravity from phenomena, and I frame no hypotheses."

Sir Isaac Newton

Keep in mind that Newton was a key figure in the Scientific Revolution, so the discipline of his methods was novel at the time.

Newton's admission of uncertainty reflects the humility and skepticism necessary for scientific inquiry.

Newton's idea serves as a reminder of the importance of rigorous observation and experimentation in the pursuit of truth. Despite his groundbreaking discoveries in the field of physics, Newton acknowledges the limits of his own understanding and refrains from speculation without sufficient evidence – another key concept of the Scientific Revolution.

MARCH 29

"The deterioration of every government begins with the decay of the principles on which it was founded."

Montesquieu

A chilling quote, when one stops to think about how we often chip away at governmental structures, with every passing generation.

Montesquieu's insight into the cycle of governance underscores the importance of upholding foundational principles and values. Political expediency often leads to short-term moves that undermine the preservation of foundational principles. This quote challenges us to remain steadfast in our commitment to truth and justice.

Spend a minute going back to the first principles of your government, and asking yourself if your political views are consistent with them.

MARCH 30

"Custom is the great guide of human life."

David Hume

Hume's idea is a reflection on the pervasive influence of tradition and habit in shaping human behavior and society.

People often rely on established norms and routines to navigate their existence. From a practical standpoint, this idea emphasizes the importance of understanding cultural and societal influences when designing products or experiences.

The counterpoint is a reminder to challenge conventional thinking and disrupt established norms when striving to create breakthroughs or any type of transformation - be it for self or for society. We can better appreciate the need to innovate and introduce new ideas that have the potential to reshape behaviors and enhance the human experience.

MARCH 31

"I dwell in possibility."

Emily Dickinson

Dickinson acknowledges the realm of imagination and potentiality, where the boundaries of reality are expanded and the horizon of possibility stretches endlessly before us. With a simple lyricism that is characteristic of her poetic genius, Dickinson chooses to "dwell" rather than merely exist, implying a deliberate immersion in the world of what could be.

The line beckons us to venture beyond the confines of the ordinary and to embrace the infinite possibilities that await us. Her words resonate with a sense of wonder and curiosity, challenging us to cultivate a mindset of openness and receptivity to the myriad paths that life may unfold before us.

We can approach today "dwelling in possibility" and be filled with hope and inspiration.

APRIL 1

"The person who has lived the most is not the one who has lived the longest, but the one with the richest experiences."

Jean-Jacques Rousseau

Rousseau seems to be saying that life should be about quality over quantity.

Each day, we have an opportunity to prioritize experiences, impact, fulfillment, and relationships over all else. It doesn't matter if we live a long time, if that time is not filled with a meaningful existence on this earth.

Rousseau urges us to cultivate a sense of curiosity and adventure, recognizing that true fulfillment arises from the richness and diversity of our lived experiences rather than just the avoidance of risk and accumulation of years.

APRIL 2

"If you have knowledge, let others light their candles in it."

Margaret Fuller

There can be an instinct to hoard knowledge, as it can be seen as power or credibility. Fuller tells us to resist that urge.

Fuller's call to share knowledge and give of yourself underscores the importance of generosity and altruism in fostering a culture of learning and enlightenment. This quote challenges us to embrace a spirit of openness and collaboration, to teach if we can and share information that can help others.

True wisdom is not diminished by sharing but rather multiplied, enriching the lives of all who partake in it. Your influence is greater when you share.

APRIL 3

"Nature is pleased with simplicity. And nature is no dummy."

Sir Isaac Newton

We see several quotes from Newton's work where he celebrates the virtues of simplicity.

Newton's recognition of nature's affinity for simplicity reflects an understanding of the underlying order and harmony in the natural world. He seems pleased by the elegance and efficiency of natural processes.

Newton's observation underscores the importance of simplicity in scientific explanation and design, emphasizing the beauty and effectiveness of solutions that are borne from the principles of nature.

APRIL **4**

"**Governments must be conformable to the nature of the governed; governments are even a result of that nature.**"

Giambattista Vico

Do organizations take on the temperament of their leader? Perhaps it is the other way around, that the leadership takes on the temperament of the participants.

Vico's assertion emphasizes the reciprocal relationship between government and society, highlighting the importance of governance that is responsive to the needs and values of its citizens.

If we actively engage in civic participation and hold their elected officials accountable for their actions, over time the government or entity will reflect the will and values of the masses. It might not happen immediately, but it will be a steady, gradual march in that direction.

APRIL 5

**"If you have built castles in the air, your work
need not be lost; that is where they should be.
Now put the foundations under them."**

Henry David Thoreau

One has to wonder if Thoreau, always the dreamer,
learned this lesson the hard way. Whatever the case, his words
remind us of the importance of translating our dreams and
aspirations into tangible action and effort.

Today's reader might be inspired by the quote to roll up
our sleeves and do the hard work necessary to turn our
dreams into reality. Success is not achieved through wishful
thinking alone but through perseverance, determination, and
a willingness to lay the groundwork for our ambitions to flourish. Much of realizing an aspirational goal or achievement is
about the details that will make it more likely to happen.

APRIL 6

"It is not from the benevolence of the butcher, the brewer, or the baker that we expect our dinner, but from their regard to their own interest."

Adam Smith

Adam Smith, and a belief in humans acting in thier self-interest, go hand-in-hand.

Smith's observation highlights the role of self-interest in driving economic activity and productivity. We sometimes overcomplicate things, especially when it comes to interactions with others, whether monetary or otherwise.

While we often try to have a noble mission associated with our work or endeavors, it is helpful to keep in mind that people are often driven by getting what they want or need, at a reasonable expense to them. Similarly, as you try to create a better life for yourself, remember that the person on the other side of the transaction is trying to do the same for them.

APRIL 7

"What Paul says about Peter tells us more about Paul than about Peter"

Baruch Spinoza

In this concise statement, Spinoza is pointing out that when someone talks about another person, they often reveal more about themselves than the person they're talking about. It might say more about their attitudes or biases than about the other person's actions or character.

We are constantly intaking more information than we can use, and this line stresses the importance of perspective and context when interpreting information about individuals. It suggests that when people describe others, their words can be influenced by their own experiences, beliefs, and feelings.

APRIL 8

**"Music is the hidden arithmetical exercise of a
mind unconscious that it is calculating."**

Gottfried Leibniz

The link between music and math is well-documented.
Here, Leibniz takes it a step further, noting that music might
be the mind's subconscious way of doing pleasing math at
length.

Leibniz's observation sheds light on the mathematical
underpinnings of music, revealing the inherent connection
between art and science. It is also a comment on the
interdisciplinary nature of human creativity.

We can remember that the left-brained and right-brained
worlds have some overlap. You don't need to be one or the
other. Even in art, there is logic, and even in data and analysis,
there is creativity.

APRIL 9

"Being all equal and independent, no one ought to harm another in his life, health, liberty, or possessions."

John Locke

A line strikingly similar to what would be written a century later in the Declaration of Independence, Locke's assertion of equality and individual rights underscores the principles of justice and human dignity that underpin a just society.

The simplicity of Locke's ideas offers a timeless ethical framework for guiding our actions.

Locke seems to be suggesting that the Golden Rule is paramount. Treat others with respect, and don't infringe on their ability to live their lives.

APRIL 10

"It is not very unreasonable that the rich should contribute to the public expense, not only in proportion to their revenue, but something more than in that proportion."

Adam Smith

An idea that has influenced countless policy discussions and is still debated to this day, Smith's perspective on progressive taxation underscores the principle of fiscal fairness and social responsibility in governance.

While Smith is often steadfast in his belief that people should be able to earn to their maximum potential without government intrusion, he also acknowledges that the wealthier of us should be asked to fund a larger share toward the greater good.

The quote urges us to recognize the moral imperative of wealth redistribution, and embrace policies that promote social justice and some level of opportunity equality.

APRIL 11

"The world of reality has its limits; the world of imagination is boundless."

Jean-Jacques Rousseau

One might argue that in today's age, the world of reality has fewer limits than it used to. Still, Rousseau's reflection on the power of imagination underscores the transformative potential of creativity and vision.

Pragmatism is valued in most fields, but the fact is that it often stifles innovation and imagination. Rousseau's idea challenges us to embrace the limitless possibilities of the human mind.

Challenge yourself to not be bound by the way things are done in today's world. "The way we've always done it" might not indeed be the best way.

APRIL 12

"Judge a man by his questions rather than by his answers."

Voltaire

Voltaire's insight underscores the importance of curiosity and inquiry in assessing a person's character and intellect. The process of questioning and exploration can tell you much about a person, particularly how sincerely they are trying to understand all sides of a subject. It can also give you clues as to their motivates and context.

Voltaire urges us to be open-minded, and have a true dialogue and exchange of ideas with others, recognizing that true wisdom arises not from having all the answers but from asking the right questions and seeking deeper insights into the nature of reality.

APRIL 13

"Nihil est sine ratione. [There is nothing without a reason.]"

Gottfried Leibniz

Leibniz's maxim highlights the principle of sufficient reason, emphasizing the underlying order and rationality within the universe. We can seek to understand the underlying reasons and causes behind events and phenomena.

By embracing a mindset of inquiry and critical thinking, individuals can gain deeper insights into the complexities of the world around them. Leibniz's wisdom encourages us to seek rational explanations and meaning amidst the apparent randomness of life, fostering a greater appreciation for the inherent order and harmony within the cosmos.

APRIL 14

"Excellence is to do a common thing in an uncommon way."

Booker T. Washington

This profound Washington quote encapsulates the essence of innovation and the relentless pursuit of greatness. It speaks to the transformative power of thinking differently, of challenging the status quo, and of pushing the boundaries of what is possible.

True excellence is not merely about replicating what has been done before, but about infusing it with creativity, passion, and originality. It is about approaching familiar tasks with fresh perspectives, uncovering new insights, and reimagining solutions in ways that inspire awe and admiration.

As you go about your day, try to take on every task - regardless of its visibility or status - with the pursuit of the utmost excellence.

APRIL 15

"If every individual be bound to society, society is equally bound to him, by a contract which from its nature equally binds both parties."

Cesare Beccaria

Beccaria's articulation of the social contract theory highlights the reciprocal obligations that exist between individuals and the societies in which they live. The social contract was a concept that many writers of the era leaned-on as they made broader points, and is one of the key outcomes of the era.

Beccaria's wisdom serves as a foundation for understanding the rights and duties of citizens. Recognize your role as active participants in the social fabric, acknowledging a duty to contribute to the common good while also holding society accountable to its obligations.

It is about reciprocity and mutual respect, and cultivating a sense of solidarity and cooperation.

APRIL 16

"Forever is composed of nows."

Emily Dickinson

This quote is the essence of existential wisdom, inviting us to contemplate the fleeting nature of time and the eternal significance of the present moment. Dickinson, known for her keen insight into the human condition, captures the complicated relationship between the transient nature of individual moments and the enduring continuum of existence.

Dickinson's efficient words remind us that the passage of time is not merely a linear progression but a mosaic of all kinds of moments and instances, each imbued with its own significance and potential. Live in the moment, and don't wish away the present.

APRIL 17

"The actions of men are the best interpreters of their thoughts."

John Locke

So many quotes from the Enlightenment leaders centered around the idea that actions speak louder than words.

Here, Locke emphasizes the significance of deeds as a reflection of one's true beliefs and intentions. Actions carry greater weight in assessing one's authenticity and integrity.

The line can be used not just for assessing others, but for evaluating ourselves. Do we live with the integrity we intend to? Do we actually do what we say is the right thing to do?

APRIL 18

"This time, like all times, is a very good one, if we but know what to do with it."

Ralph Waldo Emerson

A great example of Emerson's optimism. This is a special moment, if you have the ability to recognize it and make the most of it.

We often spend our time longing for the past or hoping for the future. Both are human nature, and part of the thought process.

What Emerson is telling us, though, is to live in the present! The present is unique and worth being savored, if you have the ability to be in the moment. As you go about your day, try to be present, try to stay in the moment.

APRIL 19

"Little else is requisite to carry a state to the highest degree of opulence from the lowest barbarism but peace, easy taxes, and a tolerable administration of justice."

Adam Smith

Smith's observation encapsulates the essence of economic prosperity – along with a fair and just society – with characteristic clarity.

Peace provides certainty and safety. Easy taxes, characterized by simplicity and fairness, minimize the burden or drag on the economy. A tolerable administration of justice ensures the protection of property rights and the enforcement of contracts.

Smith's insight outlines the formula for a government to create an environment where people can thrive economically.

APRIL 20

"Don't think money does everything or you are going to end up doing everything for money."

Voltaire

A healthy separation of money and purpose seems to be what Voltaire is advocating in this line. Voltaire's critique of materialism and the pursuit of wealth reflects his concerns about the dehumanizing effects of valuing money above all else.

In an increasingly commercialized society, where financial success often takes precedence over ethical considerations, Voltaire's words remind us of the importance of prioritizing values beyond monetary gain. His insight challenges us to resist the temptation to sacrifice integrity and happiness for material wealth.

APRIL 21

"So miserable is human destiny that the lights which deliver man from one evil throw him into another."

Pierre Bayle

Bayle's reflection on the human condition offers a sobering perspective on the paradox between progress and suffering. There are unintended consequences that often accompany human innovation.

By embracing a holistic approach to progress that considers the broader impact on society and the environment, perhaps we can navigate the complexities of modern life with greater wisdom and compassion.

Know that there are inherent trade-offs involved in human existence, and strive for a balance that promotes progress while being aware of the many slippery slopes.

APRIL 22

"The happiest people are those who do the most for others."

Booker T. Washington

If you ever needed a quote to adjust your mindset for the day, this is it.

Washington's observation that the happiest people out there are the ones who find ways to help others is echoed in countless studies on happiness that followed.

Find someone in need of help, and help them. Perhaps it is that simple. Or in a work or professional setting, see to it that as you go about your day, you are doing everything you can to make someone else's day better, whether it be a coworker, customer, student, patient, or any other person you encounter.

APRIL 23

"Aim above morality. Be not simply good, but good for something."

Henry David Thoreau

It is almost as if Thoreau was speaking to his fellow philosophers who wrote mainly about personal virtue. In this quote, he is urging us to transcend mere adherence to ethical standards and instead aspire toward a higher purpose, reminding us that our aspirations should extend beyond the boundaries of conventional goodness.

Thoreau also seems to be telling us to find purpose behind our goodness—to consider how our actions can be harnessed for the greater good of society and the world at large.

Let your good be not just inwardly-facing, but outwardly too. Ask if our actions are self-serving or if they will have some positive effect on our fellow humans.

APRIL 24

"Morality is not the doctrine of how we may make ourselves happy, but how we may make ourselves worthy of happiness."

Immanuel Kant

An interesting suggestion that we should actually add a step between morality and happiness, the step of worthiness. Kant distinguishes between morality and personal happiness in this quote. He argues that morality isn't about seeking pleasure or self-interest, but about living in a way that is deserving of happiness. Kant believed that true moral actions are motivated by duty and respect for moral law, rather than personal gain.

This quote reflects Kant's deontological ethics, which prioritize the inherent rightness or wrongness of actions over their consequences.

He would say strive to be the best, most righteous person you can. That is what you can control.

APRIL 25

"The force of character is cumulative."

Ralph Waldo Emerson

A profound, yet concise quote from Emerson.

His assertion regarding the cumulative nature of character resonates with a framework that emphasizes a constant interplay between the individual and the world around them. Identifying character as a cumulative force suggests that our personal attributes and moral dispositions are not static entities but rather emergent properties that evolve over time.

Perhaps the way to be a good, kind, impactful person is not by going out and doing one incredibly virtuous thing for the world, but by doing countless smaller kind things for people, consistently, day after day.

APRIL 26

"A man may fulfill the object of his existence by asking a question he cannot answer, and attempting a task he cannot achieve."

Oliver Wendell Holmes

Holmes encourages us to embrace uncertainty and challenges we are bound to encounter in life as opportunities for growth and self-discovery.

You might discover that you can find meaning and purpose in the pursuit of the unknown, or a goal that may seem largely unattainable. The journey is the reward as the Chinese proverb says, and the pursuit of an answer or an objective, even if not attained, can yield life experience that proves irreplaceable.

In short, challenge yourself, because it will make you better.

APRIL 27

"The rules of morality are not the conclusion of our reason."

David Hume

Hume seems to suggest that morality is not a logical deduction or a product of rational analysis alone. Instead, it is deeply rooted in human nature, shaped by our emotions, instincts, and cultural influences.

The rules of morality often emerge from our collective experiences and shared values, evolving over time through social interactions and historical context. While reason plays a role in understanding and interpreting moral principles, it is our innate sense of empathy and social cohesion that ultimately guides our ethical behavior.

To fully grasp the complexities of morality, look beyond pure reason and consider the intricate interplay of emotions, societal norms, and personal experiences that contribute to our moral framework.

APRIL 28

"Our Business here is not to know all things, but those which concern our conduct."

John Locke

Locke's reflection on the scope of human knowledge speaks to the importance of prioritizing practical wisdom in our pursuits. This line is about focus, and learning to discern the noise from the signal.

It can be tempting to meddle in matters that aren't relevant to your life or your pursuits. Resist the urge - it simply takes energy away from the things you are working toward.

Locke's insight offers a reminder to focus on what truly matters in shaping our lives. Focus on acquiring knowledge that matters, and fosters personal growth. Try to leave the noise for others.

APRIL 29

"The perilous time for the most highly gifted is not youth.... the perilous season is middle age, when a false wisdom tempts them to doubt the divine origin of the dreams of their youth; when the world comes to them, not with the song of the siren, against which all books warn us, but as a wise old man counseling acquiescence in what is below them."

Elizabeth Peabody

Peabody's insight into the journey of someone with gifts and talents resonates deeply with the struggles many face as they navigate the complexities of life. She illustrates the paradox of middle age, where the allure of so-called common sense threatens to water-down the divine inspiration that once fueled one's dreams.

The line is a cautionary tale against the seductive whispers of complacency, conformity, and settling that can dim brilliant aspirations.

APRIL 30

"To write a good love letter, you ought to begin without knowing what you mean to say, and to finish without knowing what you have written."

Jean-Jacques Rousseau

An interesting lesson in writing from the heart. Rousseau's advice on writing a love letter emphasizes the spontaneity and sincerity of genuine expression.

Rousseau's wisdom reminds us of the power of authentic connection and vulnerability in relationships. To learn from this quote, individuals can embrace authenticity and emotional honesty in their communication with loved ones, allowing their words to flow freely from the heart rather than adhering to rigid conventions or expectations.

When writing from the heart, try to capture your emotion and don't think too much about structure. Let it flow!

MAY 1

"Parents wonder why the streams are bitter, when they themselves poison the fountain."

John Locke

Locke wrote often about the influence of our environment and contacts on our character and morals, and here he examines the family dynamic. Specifically, Locke is arguing that nurture may be more powerful than nature.

Locke's reflection on parenting highlights the importance of leading by example and fostering a nurturing and constructive environment for children, and a reminder of the responsibility that comes with parenthood.

As a parent, cultivate self-awareness and strive to embody the virtues you wish to instill in their children. By modeling empathy, integrity, and kindness in your own actions, your children will likely emulate many aspects of how you are living.

MAY 2

"The highest activity a human being can attain is learning for understanding, because to understand is to be free."

Baruch Spinoza

Spinoza's insight into the liberating power of understanding underscores the transformative potential of knowledge in shaping our lives. Spinoza's wisdom offers a compelling reminder of the importance of deep intellectual inquiry.

Don't view learning as just a lesson on how to do something or memorization of facts. Instead, embrace lifelong learning as a means of personal growth and empowerment.

By seeking to comprehend the complexities of the world and the human experience, we can turn away from ignorance and prejudice, fostering greater autonomy and self-realization and more personal fulfillment.

MAY 3

"Why is there something rather than nothing?"

Gottfried Leibniz

A quote that strikes at the heart of our human curiosity and wonder. It's the kind of question that lingers in the back of our minds, stirring a sense of awe and contemplation about the nature of existence itself.

Put simply, Leibniz is asking why the universe exists at all, instead of just being void and empty. It's a profound inquiry that transcends religious, philosophical, and scientific boundaries, prompting us to ponder the mysteries of creation and the origins of life.

Whether you're a theologian pondering divine creation, a philosopher musing on the nature of reality, or a scientist exploring the laws of physics, this question remains a timeless enigma—a reminder of the boundless mysteries that lie beyond our understanding.

MAY 4

**"God be thanked for books; they are the voices
of the distant and the dead, and make us heirs
of the spiritual life of past ages. "**

William Ellery Channing

A beautiful thing about books is that it allows you to learn from people who it would have been impossible to meet, people who lived decades and centuries before you.

Channing's reflection on the value of books underscores the transformative power of literature in enriching our lives and broadening our perspectives. Books carry timeless wisdom and insight, lessons th at in a world of only verbal history may be lost.

Through books, we can connect with the thoughts, experiences, and aspirations of great thinkers of the past, enriching our understanding of ourselves and the world around us.

MAY 5

"The soul should always stand ajar, ready to welcome the ecstatic experience."

Emily Dickinson

Do you live with an open mind, and an open soul?

Dickinson's metaphorical imagery encourages us to remain open to the transformative power of life's most profound moments. This quote challenges us to cultivate a sense of curiosity, receptivity and awe. It urges us to embrace the full spectrum of human experience, from the mundane to the sublime, recognizing that true fulfillment arises from being fully present to the richness of life.

Dickinson is always about hope and optimism, and those traits are more to exist in someone ready to embrace the world, and let it in.

MAY 6

"All wealth is the product of labor."

John Locke

A passage that resembles something you might have read from Adam Smith.

Locke's assertion underscores the intrinsic link between effort and prosperity, challenging notions of entitlement and privilege. Locke suggests that wealth always comes from work of some sort.

Going economic for a second, we should point out that the Marxist Labor Theory of Value would back up the notion of wealth and labor being tied together. However, others have suggested that value can be added in other ways, through creativity and ownership.

MAY 7

"The price of anything is the amount of life you exchange for it. "

Henry David Thoreau

Many of Thoreau's lines can hit hard, and this one has likely driven some serious self-reflection in many. He offers a profound perspective on the true cost of our choices and pursuits in life, and that the tradeoff is often between doing an endeavor and trading some of your precious time on earth for it.

Instead of equating success with material possessions or wealth, consider the deeper implications of our decisions. It challenges us to reflect on how we allocate our time, energy, and resources, and to prioritize the things that truly matter to us.

By valuing experiences – and our time – over possessions, relationships over status, and purpose over profit, we enrich our lives and cultivate a deeper sense of meaning and fulfillment.

MAY 8

"The brain is wider than the sky."

Emily Dickinson

Dickinson's metaphorical comparison emphasizes the boundless capacity of the human mind. The limitless possibilities of thought and imagination inside one's mind are more profound than even the physical universe.

This quote encourages us to embrace the power of creativity and innovation, recognizing that true progress and discovery arise from the expansive horizons of the human intellect.

Regardless of what kind of constraints might seem to exist, the frontiers within one's own mind are endless. We should not forget to think and imagine.

MAY 9

"The less men think, the more they talk."

Montesquieu

Montesquieu encapsulates a timeless truth about the relationship between thought and speech, highlighting the tendency for verbosity to fill the void left by intellectual stagnation.

With a clarity that cuts through the chatter, Montesquieu exposes the curious nature of human communication, suggesting that the proliferation of words often masks a dearth of substantive thought.

We see this all the time in the present day – communication channels are often dominated by the people or content that are heavy on volume or charge but light on reflection or originality.

Perhaps Montesquieu's challenge to us is to spend more time forming sound ideas, and less time sharing half-baked ones.

MAY 10

"I have learned that to be with those I like is enough"

Walt Whitman

There comes a point for many where the priority shifts

from achievement, image, or external success to simply spending time with the people who enjoy spending time with.

Whitman's line is a reflection of the significance of surrounding oneself with like-minded individuals who inspire and support personal growth, and a reminder to prioritize quality over quantity in relationships, emphasizing the profound impact of positive social interactions on overall well-being and happiness.

MAY 11

"The murder that is depicted as a horrible crime is repeated in cold blood, remorselessly."

Cesare Beccaria

In this chilling quote from Beccaria, he highlights the paradoxical nature of depicting murder as a heinous crime while simultaneously perpetuating it through calculated, unrepentant actions. He suggests that sensationalizing murder as a horrific act can inadvertently desensitize individuals to its gravity, leading to its repetition without remorse.

Beccaria's words serve as a sobering reminder of the potential consequences of glorifying violence or treating it lightly in society. They urge reflection on the ways in which attitudes towards crime and punishment can influence behavior, emphasizing the need for a balanced and compassionate approach to addressing criminal behavior.

MAY 12

"It is not the young people that degenerate; they are not spoiled till those of mature age are already sunk into corruption."

Montesquieu

The young can get a bad rap, but Montesquieu's insight is that the bigger risk is those who are older. A concept later shared by 19th century American Elizabeth Peabody, Montesquieu notes that older generations ultimately enable the transgressions of the entire society.

Moral decay often stems from the example set by those in positions of authority, and this quote challenges us to lead by example. It urges us to not let the power or influence that might come later in life cause our judgment or morals to deteriorate.

Perhaps if the rich, established, and powerful can keep their moral clarity and virtue, the entire society will.

MAY 13

"When a man is prey to his emotions, he is not his own master."

Baruch Spinoza

Spinoza's line has hints of the Stoic thinking that prevailed nearly 2,000 years before him. His insight into the nature of emotional mastery offers a valuable lesson in self-control and self-mastery.

Spinoza's wisdom serves as a reminder of the importance of emotional regulation. Cultivate mindfulness and self-awareness, learning to recognize and manage their emotions effectively. By developing the capacity to respond thoughtfully rather than react impulsively, individuals can regain control over their lives and make wise decisions that align with their values and goals. When you are angry, you have lost control.

MAY 14

"The condition of man... is a condition of war of everyone against everyone."

Thomas Hobbes

While the Enlightenment thinkers tended to be optimistic, Hobbes had a bleak streak in him.

Hobbes's assessment of human nature highlights the inherent conflict and competition that pervade society. Self-interest often trumps cooperation, this quote challenges us to recognize the fragility of social order. It urges us to strive for peace and harmony through mutual understanding and compromise, recognizing that true progress arises from collective efforts to transcend our primal instincts.

This line perhaps sets up the need for a social contract, the concept written about by so many others of the time.

MAY 15

"To be yourself in a world that is constantly trying to make you something else is the greatest accomplishment."

Ralph Waldo Emerson

A common thread of transcendentalist thinking is that we shouldn't conform just for the sake of conforming. Emerson extols the virtue of authenticity and self-acceptance in a society that often pressures us to conform to societal norms or expectations, in a quote that reminds us of something Thoreau might write.

Given today's relentless pursuit of external validation, this quote serves as a powerful reminder to stay true to our unique identities, values, and aspirations. Resist the temptation to mold ourselves into someone we're not and to embrace our individuality with confidence and pride, knowing that our true worth lies in being authentically ourselves.

MAY 16

"Your glass will not do you half so much service as a serious reflection on your own minds."

Mary Astell

Does the quick buzz of a chemical make you feel more enlightened? Astell might argue that it is fleeting compared to the depth you will attain from true, dedicated thinking.

By encouraging individuals to engage in deep introspection and critical self-reflection, Astell underscores the value of introspective inquiry in gaining insight into one's thoughts, feelings, and motivations.

Let's not let days go by without practicing deep thought. It could be on a particular topic, or on matters in general.

MAY 17

"I prefer liberty with danger than peace with slavery."

Jean-Jacques Rousseau

Personal liberty was such an important central concept in the Enlightenment, and Rousseau's affirmation of the value of liberty underscores the enduring relevance of individual freedom in the face of oppression.

Rousseau's wisdom serves as a rallying cry for those who seek to resist tyranny and uphold the principles of democracy. The fact is that with freedom comes some risk. It can be unpredictable, but that is the worthwhile price to pay in order to not be controlled by others.

MAY 18

"Hell is truth seen too late."

Thomas Hobbes

Hobbes's warning speaks to the consequences of ignorance and denial in the face of reality. Truth often takes a backseat to comfort and convenience, and the path of least resistance. This quote challenges us to confront uncomfortable truths head-on. It urges us to embrace honesty and transparency in our relationships and endeavors, recognizing that true liberation arises from the courage to confront the harsh realities of existence.

Hobbes is noting that having a clear picture of the truth emerge – but at a point too late to do anything about it – can be agonizing. It is better to relentlessly pursue truth the entire time, so you don't find yourself in that difficult position.

MAY 19

"He who does not act does not exist."

Gottfried Leibniz

Such a simple quote that drives home a factor of our very existence.

Leibniz's aphorism underscores the existential significance of action in defining one's existence and identity. Multiple times, we see Leibniz point out the need for not just thought, but action. Without it, you are not impacting the world as you could.

It begs a question for us to ask ourselves every day: Are you translating your ideas into action? Are the ideals in your head making their way to some sort of impact? If not, think about how you can make it so.

MAY 20

"Common sense is judgment without reflection, shared by an entire class, an entire nation, or the entire human race."

Giambattista Vico

Could it be that what is often referred to as common sense is simply groupthink?

Vico's observation sheds light on the collective nature of common sense and its influence on societal norms and beliefs.

To learn from this quote, perhaps we should work on our critical thinking skills and question the validity of commonly held beliefs. Doing some independent reflection and analysis, individuals can develop a more nuanced understanding of complex issues and resist the influence of group mentality. You might find that while others zig, you should zag.

MAY 21

**"The colour of the skin is in no way connected
with strength of the mind or intellectual
powers."**

Benjamin Banneker

A line that, when it was written, sadly might have been
viewed with skepticism by many. Banneker was living during
the slave era in America, but in Maryland which was a free
state.

Banneker's assertion challenges the prevailing notions of
the time of racial superiority and inferiority. By emphasizing
the fundamental equality of all individuals, regardless of race
or ethnicity, he advocates for a more inclusive and equitable
vision of humanity.

This quote serves as a powerful rebuke to the injustices of
racism and discrimination which he lived through, urging
readers to recognize and celebrate the inherent worth and
dignity of every human being.

MAY 22

"I would warn you that I do not attribute to nature either beauty or deformity, order or confusion. Only in relation to our imagination can things be called beautiful or ugly, well-ordered or confused."

Baruch Spinoza

Are things inherently beautiful or ugly, or is it all in how we view them? The subjective filter that our senses and perception applies to everything we interact with and colors how we see them.

By recognizing that beauty and order are subjective constructs shaped by cultural conditioning and personal bias, individuals can embrace a more inclusive and tolerant worldview.

200 years later, Margaret Wolfe Hungerford would write "Beauty is in the eye of the beholder" which has become a common refrain ever since.

MAY 23

"Happy is the nation without a history"

Cesare Beccaria

In this striking quote by Beccaria, he suggests that a nation without a history of conflicts or turmoil is a fortunate one. He implies that a lack of historical events, particularly negative ones, can lead to greater happiness and stability within a society.

The quote challenges us to consider the role of history in shaping individuals and societies. It prompts reflection on how past events, both positive and negative, influence the present and future. While Beccaria's statement may seem idealistic, it also serves as a reminder of the importance of striving for peace and harmony in the collective narrative of a nation.

MAY 24

"We are like chameleons, we take our hue and the color of our moral character, from those who are around us."

John Locke

Locke foreshadows a concept that has gained popularity in recent times, that we are the average of the five people we spend the most time with.

Here, Locke's analogy underscores the profound influence of the social environment on character and individual morality. Having an internal moral compass is important, but you are no doubt influenced by the people you interact with and trust.

Perhaps the learning here is to choose your friends carefully, and if one has values or morals counter to good living, consider easing them out of your world.

MAY 25

"A mind that is stretched by a new experience can never go back to its old dimensions."

Oliver Wendell Holmes

In this quote, Holmes emphasizes the transformative power of new experiences on the human mind. He suggests that exposure to new ideas, people, and situations can expand one's perspective and understanding in ways that are irreversible.

This idea aligns with Holmes' belief in the importance of lifelong learning and intellectual curiosity. Throughout his own life, Holmes pursued a wide range of interests, from law and literature to science and philosophy, embodying the idea that the mind is enriched by constant exploration and growth.

You can take Holmes' lesson, and always keep expanding your thinking. If you do, it will permanently be broader and more informed than it was before.

MAY 26

"Reading furnishes the mind only with materials of knowledge; it is thinking that makes what we read ours."

John Locke

Locke's imagery of raw materials versus a finished product is astute.

Locke highlights the crucial distinction between passive consumption of information and active engagement with ideas. To truly internalize and apply knowledge, one must engage in deep thinking and introspection.

As you read, remember, intaking information is good, but it is only the first step. As Marcus Aurelius suggested, synthesize information and then do something with it.

MAY 27

"Love consists in desiring to give what is our own to another and feeling his delight as our own."

Emmanuel Swedenborg

Swedenborg's timeless wisdom reminds us of the transformative power of selfless love and empathy in today's fast-paced and often disconnected world. It is human nature to be jealous or envious, but can you rise above and feel the joy of making another person truly happy and grateful?

Swedenborg challenges us to strive to gain true joy from giving to others and find fulfillment in acts of generosity and compassion, recognizing that true happiness from the joy of giving and sharing in the joy of others.

The quote reinforces that love is not merely an emotion, but a choice—a choice to extend ourselves for the benefit of others, and in doing so, experience the true depth and richness of life.

MAY 28

"The real price of everything, what everything really costs to the man who wants to acquire it, is the toil and trouble of acquiring it."

Adam Smith

Perhaps the foremost economic thinker of the Enlightenment Era, Adam Smith, asserts that the true cost or "real price" of any commodity or service is measured by the effort and labor required to obtain it, the human exertion behind economic transactions. This quote resonates with themes of personal sacrifice and opportunity costs within economic decision-making.

When paying for something, you aren't just exchanging money for a good, service, or experience. You are exchanging whatever it took to obtain that money -- time, patience, effort, valued possessions, etc. Money is just the way we conveniently measure it all.

MAY 29

"Curiosity is the lust of the mind."

Thomas Hobbes

Hobbes's characterization of curiosity as a form of desire underscores the power of intellectual inquiry.

It is a playful quote, as lust is often viewed as a negative – as one of Christianity's seven deadly sins. In this context, however, Hobbes suggests that lust of the mind - the desire to know and understand things that you don't yet - is not bad. In fact, curiosity is typically seen as a virtue.

Indulge your mind's lust for understanding, and be curious. Explore the world, learn new things.

MAY 30

"The strongest is never strong enough to be always the master, unless he transforms strength into right, and obedience into duty."

Jean-Jacques Rousseau

Rousseau spent lots of time thinking about social power, and in this quote he recognizes the nuanced relationship between power, authority, and legitimacy.

The line suggests that raw strength alone will not be a sustainable advantage, and is insufficient to maintain lasting dominance or leadership. True mastery requires transforming mere physical or coercive strength into moral authority and just governance.

The best leaders and citizens strive past strength to attain the more difficult aims of fairness, justice, and the common good, thereby turning obedience into a sense of duty and obligation rather than mere submission to force.

MAY 31

"I am of the African race, and in the color which is natural to them of the deepest dye; and it is under a sense of the most profound gratitude to the Supreme Ruler of the Universe."

Benjamin Banneker

Banneker poetically references his skin color and then puts it in the context of the human race. His expression of pride in his African heritage reflects his defiance against the prevailing racism and prejudice of his time.

There is a lesson we can all take from Banneker - to embrace our identity and heritage with dignity and pride. It is a powerful affirmation of African American identity and resilience, written during the slavery era in America,, inspiring readers to celebrate and honor their cultural heritage.

JUNE 1

"The nature of heaven is to provide a place there for all who lead good lives, no matter what their religion may be."

Emmanuel Swedenborg

Swedenborg spent lots of time thinking about heaven, and his inclusive vision of heaven challenges us to embrace a broader understanding of spirituality and recognize the common humanity that unites us all.

These words were no doubt challenged by others at the time, as many denominations were becoming more strict and even less tolerant.

Swedenborg insists that the quality of our character and the sincerity of our actions is what matters. We can use this lesson as part of our daily mindset, but also as a mindset of tolerance as we interact with others.

JUNE 2

"Optimism is the madness of insisting that all is well when we are miserable."

Voltaire

A cynical quote from Voltaire, and one that reminds us to root ourselves in reality.

Voltaire's critique of blind optimism reflects his skepticism towards unwarranted positivity in the face of adversity.

Voltaire witnessed firsthand the consequences of blind faith and unwarranted optimism. His words caution against dismissing legitimate grievances and personal suffering under the guise of relentless positivity, urging us to confront reality with clarity and courage rather than denying its complexities.

JUNE 3

"Revolt is the right of the people"

John Locke

The right to revolt is a principle of liberty and self-determination, and an underpinning to democratic societies.

Movements for social justice and political reform are part of the gradual progression toward a better, fairer world. Locke's insight offers a timeless reminder of the importance of standing up for one's rights and freedoms.

While not directly calling it out, Locke might be encouraging civic engagement and advocating for positive change. While revolt can mean a dramatic protest, it can also mean thoughtful dissent and peaceful actions aligned with causes or issues important at the global or local levels.

JUNE 4

"Such as the love is, such is the wisdom, consequently such is the man."

Emmanuel Swedenborg

-Emmanuel Swedenborg

Swedenborg's profound insight into the interconnectedness of love, wisdom, and character challenges us to examine the quality of our intentions and actions.

This quote serves as a reminder that true greatness is defined not by external achievements or accolades, but by the depth of our character and the sincerity of our intentions. It encourages us to prioritize the cultivation of virtues such as compassion, empathy, and integrity, recognizing that these qualities are the true measure of a person's worth. It reminds us that true wisdom arises from the heart, not the mind, and that the path to greatness lies in the cultivation of love and virtue.

JUNE 5

"Doubt is the origin of wisdom"

Rene Descartes

Being a skeptic can often cause one to ask the questions required to discover new truths.

In this quote, Descartes implies that there is benefit in not blindly accepting things as they are, but asking "why?" Curiosity often leads to examination and testing of assumptions, which in turn lead to new ideas, discoveries, or perspectives.

If you find yourself doubting something or someone, use it as a platform to inquire, be curious, and ask good questions. The result may be a more thoughtful point of view, arriving closer to a truth, or advancing your own wisdom.

JUNE 6

"Out of timber so crooked as that from which man is made, nothing entirely straight can be carved."

Immanuel Kant

Kant acknowledges the inherent imperfections of human nature. He suggests that due to our flawed nature, it's impossible to achieve absolute perfection or moral purity. This quote reflects Kant's realism about human limitations and the complexities of moral decision-making. It reminds us to be realistic in our expectations of ourselves and others, and to strive for progress rather than perfection.

Know that you have flaws and imperfections, and so does everyone else you encounter in this world. The goal is to work through the flaws, and constantly strive to be a better person. Our imperfections are laid bare, we all have them. Nobody is perfect.

JUNE 7

"The wealth of a nation depends not only on the abundance of its resources but also on the productivity of its labor."

Adam Smith

Smith tended to be pretty cerebral, and of the Enlightenment thinkers we profile, probably the one who goes deepest into his subject matter. But there is no doubt that his influence on the Age of Enlightenment was just as profound as the philosophers.

In this quote, he notes that a nation can't just rely on natural resources like farmland, timber, precious metals, or waterways. It also needs citizens who can be productive and contribute to the economy.

This concept is probably more true today than when he wrote it in the 1700s.

JUNE 8

"Truth springs from argument amongst friends."

David Hume

Hume's observation highlights the importance of open dialogue and debate in the pursuit of truth and understanding. It is a profound endorsement of collaborative discourse and intellectual exchange.

This quote underscores the importance of fostering an environment where diverse viewpoints are welcomed and respected, particularly among trusted colleagues and peers. When friends engage in constructive debate and challenge each other's perspectives, they create an opportunity to uncover deeper truths and insights that may not be apparent at first glance.

Friends, inherently, tend to trust each other, opening the door for a more honest examination of disagreements and perspectives.

JUNE 9

"Except our own thoughts, there is nothing absolutely in our power."

René Descartes

Descartes' assertion underscores a profound insight into the nature of human agency and autonomy. In these few words, Descartes challenges conventional notions of control and mastery, suggesting that true power lies not in external possessions or circumstances, but in the realm of our own thoughts and perceptions.

As we grapple with questions of identity, authenticity, and agency in an increasingly interconnected world, Descartes' emphasis on the primacy of internal thought processes offers a compelling framework for understanding the complexities of human existence.

In difficult times, where so many things seem outside your control, be comforted in knowing that your thoughts and consciousness are completely within your control.

JUNE 10

"Our dreams drench us in senses, and senses step us again in dreams."

Amos Alcott

A quote that beautifully captures the interplay between our dreams and our senses. Dreams immerse us in vivid sensory experiences, creating worlds that feel as real as waking life. In our sleep, we can see, hear, smell, and touch with an intensity that sometimes surpasses reality, showing how powerful and immersive our inner world can be.

The sights, sounds, and sensations we encounter during the day find their way into our dreams, creating a continuous loop between our lived experiences and our dream world.

Listen to your dreams. They often draw from a subconscious well of wisdom that only you have.

JUNE 11

"We do need to realize, though, that it is the quality of our love that determines the quality of this life."

Emmanuel Swedenborg

Swedenborg emphasizes the centrality of love as a guiding force in our experiences and relationships. Rather than focusing solely on external circumstances or material possessions, the richness and fulfillment of life are ultimately determined by the depth and authenticity of our connections with others. In essence, the quote invites us to prioritize cultivating love, compassion, and empathy in our interactions, recognizing their transformative power to imbue our lives with meaning, purpose, and joy.

As you go about your day, focus on the connection you have with the people you encounter, especially those important to you. Everything else might just seem like a bunch of props.

JUNE 12

"I desire to live in peace and to continue the life I have begun under the motto 'to live well you must live unseen"

René Descartes

This Descartes quote is such a departure from today's day and age, with social media, influencers, and constant connectivity.

While self-promotion and validation-seeking can be partially human nature, Descartes reminds us that there is also value and fulfillment from solitude. Thinking, exploring, and being without anyone else knowing about it can be both refreshing and healthy.

Are you taking time to be "unseen"? If not, perhaps it is time for an experiment in doing so.

JUNE 13

"I do not know how to teach philosophy without becoming a disturber of the peace."

Baruch Spinoza

Philosophy is about questioning assumptions, and examining the truth. Spinoza seems to argue that if you set out to question and examine, you better be ready to take issue with the way the world works.

Spinoza's acknowledgment of the disruptive nature of philosophical inquiry speaks to the transformative potential of critical thinking and intellectual exploration.

We think Spinoza would want you to engage with uncomfortable truths and explore alternative perspectives, even if it means disrupting the peace of established norms or the way things have always been done. Advancing knowledge and promoting critical thinking in society requires curiosity, skepticism, and in some cases disrupting the common way of thinking.

JUNE 14

"If a man will begin with certainties, he shall end in doubts; but if he will be content to begin with doubts, he shall end in certainties."

Francis Bacon

- Francis Bacon

Bacon's observation on the nature of inquiry challenges us to embrace uncertainty as a pathway to deeper understanding and certainty.

Keep in mind, Bacon was writing during the Enlightenment Era when the scientific method was becoming popular. The idea of asking a question - via a hypothesis - and then trying to prove it right or wrong with an open mind was a departure from the days of blind dogma.

Bacon's words remind us of the importance of intellectual humility and curiosity, urging us to embrace doubt as a catalyst for growth and discovery. Any time you feel completely certain about something, check yourself.

JUNE 15

"The bravest of individuals is the one who obeys his or her conscience."

James Freeman Clarke

We often view bravery as how you stand up to external people or forces, but James Freeman Clarke asserts that the hardest thing to do is to respect your own conscience.

Clarke's observation highlights the importance of moral courage and integrity in navigating life's complexities and uncertainties. Conformity and expediency create pressure on which actions to take, but this quote challenges us to listen to the voice of conscience and to stand up for what is right, even in the face of opposition or adversity.

Moral clarity begets bravery.

JUNE 16

"Beauty crowds me till I die."

Emily Dickinson

In a quote that could be more relevant today than when she wrote it, Dickinson captures the overwhelming intensity of aesthetic experience and the profound impact it exerts on the human soul.

In reading the full context of the poem, which is also named *Beauty Crowds Me Till I Die*, Dickinson seems to note that beauty can be enthralled, invigorating, and beautiful, but at some point can be oppressive, overwhelming and even suffocating.

Perhaps she is saying that beauty in the world is a wonderful thing, but like anything else, simplicity is often better than extravagance. Enjoy small encounters with beauty, but don't become disillusioned by it.

JUNE 17

**"What lies behind us and what lies before us
are tiny matters compared to what lies
within us."**

Ralph Waldo Emerson

Our internal strength and character far outweigh external circumstances. Emerson is reminding us that our soul, conscience, and internal compass and drive should be more powerful than the environment around us.

It is human nature to benchmark against others and focus on external achievements and accolades, but this quote encourages us to cultivate our inner virtues and resilience, recognizing that they are the true sources of our power and fulfillment.

Stay true to who you are, and strive to make the person inside as good as possible.

JUNE 18

"Truth emerges more readily from error than from confusion."

Francis Bacon

Bacon's reflection on the relationship between truth and error challenges us to embrace failure and adversity as opportunities for growth and learning.

Bacon was an early enthusiast of the scientific method. He knew that while proving something right was desirable, we can learn as much from proving that something is not so, or by ruling out what was once a plausible hypothesis.

The least useful, in his opinion, was confusion, vagueness, and unclarity, where nothing can be truly proven or disproven. You are much better off having a failed experiment, and learning from the experience.

JUNE 19

"Our bravest and best lessons are not learned through success, but through misadventure."

Amos Alcott

You have probably heard it said that one learns more from failure than from success.

Alcott's reflection on the value of adversity underscores the transformative power of failure and setbacks in shaping our character and resilience. We can embrace failure as a natural part of the learning process, as long as we draw lessons from it – or simply carry new resilience going forward.

It can be difficult, but view failure not as weakness or defeat, but as an opportunity for growth and self-discovery.

JUNE 20

"Many a man is praised for his reserve and so-called shyness when he is simply too proud to risk making a fool of himself."

Joseph Priestley

Priestley's observation on the nature of reserve and shyness challenges us to reconsider the motivations behind our behavior. In Priestley's era, societal norms often lauded reticence and modesty, viewing them as virtues of character. However, Priestley suggests that such behavior may stem not from humility, but from pride, timidness, and fear of judgment.

Priestly suggests that instead of adopting a reserved demeanor to protect egos and avoid vulnerability, be bold even if you might be wrong.

Don't be afraid to embrace vulnerability, and be comfortable being judged, in your pursuit for truth and impact.

JUNE 21

"The exercise of one coercion always makes another inevitable."

Anders Chydenius

This passage has strong tones of the "slippery slope" phenomenon.

In this succinct observation, Chydenius highlights the cyclical nature of coercion within society. He argues that the use of force to impose authority inevitably begets further coercion, creating a self-perpetuating cycle of oppression.

By pointing out that the one wrong by a government likely leads to more wrongs, Chydenius underscores the importance of promoting a society built on principles of consent and voluntary cooperation, where coercion is minimized, and individual liberty is maximized.

JUNE 22

"To different minds, the same world is a hell, and a heaven."

Ralph Waldo Emerson

The power of perspective.

Emerson's insight into the subjective nature of perception challenges us to recognize the power of perspective in shaping our experiences of the world. In Emerson's era, societal divisions and ideological conflicts often led to starkly contrasting interpretations of reality. Perhaps the same could be said of the present-day!

Today, echo chambers and filter bubbles so often reinforce entrenched beliefs and ideologies. The importance for empathy and open-mindedness has never been greater.

Approach everyone you interact with with an open mind. Try to understand their perspective rather than forcing yours upon them.

JUNE 23

"The job of the artist is always to deepen the mystery."

Francis Bacon

Art is a way to escape. Bacon notes that an important role of art is to challenge conventional wisdom and expand our perceptions of reality, not simply replicate what we see or think.

Moving art tends to explore the depths of human experience and emotion. Through their work, artists invite us to engage with life's mysteries and complexities in new and profound ways.

Next time you are interpreting any form of art, remember to let it take you on a journey, let it raise new questions and make new connections in your mind.

JUNE 24

**"The more elaborate our means of communi-
cation, the less we communicate."**

Joseph Priestley

This quote often resonates with present-day readers, given the hyperconnected world and information overload we have created for ourselves.

Remember, Priestley wrote this when printing presses and newspapers had just revolutionized the dissemination of information and ideas, yet Priestley suggests that such innovations may hinder genuine communication by fostering superficiality and disconnection.

The digital age increases the amount of communication we are able to do by orders of magnitude, but does it make our communication better? Don't ever overlook the need for quality in your communications – not just quantity.

JUNE 25

"Immaturity is the incapacity to use one's intelligence without the guidance of another."

Immanuel Kant

Kant is highlighting the importance of intellectual independence and self-reliance in this quote. He argues that immaturity isn't just about age, but about the inability to think for oneself and make reasoned decisions. This idea ties into Kant's broader philosophy of Enlightenment, which emphasizes the importance of individuals thinking critically and autonomously rather than blindly following authority figures or tradition.

As you get comfortable with your own ideas and reasoning, you will mature and create confidence in your ability to think. This maturity enables freedom of mind - strive for it!

JUNE 26

"I do not know what I may appear to the world; but to myself I seem to have been only like a boy playing on the seashore, and diverting myself in now and then finding a smoother pebble or a prettier shell than ordinary, whilst the great ocean of truth lay all undiscovered before me."

Sir Isaac Newton

-Sir Isaac Newton

Newton offers a profound admission on the nature of self-awareness and the pursuit of knowledge.

Despite the fleeting moments of satisfaction in discovering new "knowledge — smoother pebbles" or "prettier shells," we remain very aware of the vast expanse of undiscovered truth that lies beyond our reach.

Your perspective is a tiny fraction of the experience and knowledge in the world, and a little humility will keep you curious.

JUNE 27

"Be not astonished at new ideas; for it is well known to you that a thing does not therefore cease to be true because it is not accepted by many."

Baruch Spinoza

In this thought-provoking quote, Spinoza encourages us not to be surprised by new ideas. He reminds us that just because something isn't widely accepted doesn't mean it's not true. Spinoza urges us to keep an open mind and consider the possibility that truth can exist outside of popular opinion.

This Spinoza quote emphasizes the importance of critical thinking and independent judgment. It suggests that just because an idea isn't mainstream doesn't mean it invalid, and that we should explore new ideas that might not be widely accepted, even if those perspectives challenge conventional wisdom.

JUNE 28

"Trust thyself: every heart vibrates to that iron string."

Ralph Waldo Emerson

Self-trust and intuition were viewed as key values in the transcendentalist philosophy, and as guiding forces in navigating life's uncertainties and complexities.

This line encourages us to tune into our inner wisdom and instincts, recognizing that we possess the innate capacity to discern truth and make sound decisions. We can each follow the path that resonates most deeply with our authentic selves, knowing that it will ultimately lead us towards fulfillment and purpose.

JUNE 29

"If I have seen further it is by standing on the shoulders of giants."

Sir Isaac Newton

This might be Newton's most famous quote, and one which people neglect to attribute to him.

Newton's acknowledgment of his debt to those who came before him speaks to the humility necessary for true greatness. It reminds us of the importance of building upon the work of others and recognizing the contributions of those who paved the way.

We like to think his reference to "giants" reflects the reverence for intellectual tradition prevalent during the Enlightenment, a period marked by a collective effort to expand the boundaries of human knowledge.

Find your giants, and build upon what you have learned from them.

JUNE 30

"Such truth, as opposeth no man's profit, nor pleasure, is to all men welcome."

Thomas Hobbes

Said a little differently, a truth that doesn't conflict with anyone's gain or enjoyment is something everyone is happy to accept.

This statement underscores the intrinsic value of truth as a guiding principle for human understanding and moral action. Truths which align with the common good and uphold principles of justice and virtue are inherently welcomed by all individuals, regardless of their personal preferences or agendas.

As you interact with others, keep in mind that as long as people can pursue their livelihood and happiness as they wish, they likely will be agreeable on other matters.

JULY 1

"Ignorance and a narrow education lay the foundation of vice, and imitation and custom rear it up."

Mary Astell

An insightful observation on how negative forces are taught and reinforced in the world, and why they can be so difficult to correct.

Mary Astell's insight highlights the role of education and social influence in shaping individual character and behavior. Ignorance and narrow-mindedness are root causes of vice, and our social structures tend to reinforce those qualities as people do things the way they have always been done.

Conversely, Astell seems to be advocating for us to keep our education broad, and challenge customs when they do not make any sense.

JULY 2

"Tact is the knack of making a point without making an enemy."

Sir Isaac Newton

What a timeless quote by Newton, and one that we humans still have not entirely mastered.

Newton's insight into the importance of tact underscores the significance of effective communication and interpersonal relations. They serve as a reminder of the diplomatic skills necessary for navigating complex social dynamics.

Perhaps the words encourage us to approach interactions with others with empathy and understanding, recognizing the power of tact in building bridges and fostering mutual respect.

Ask yourself, is the goal to prove the other person wrong? Or to have meaningful dialogue with that person in a longer-term mutual pursuit of truth?

JULY 3

"Education begins the gentleman, but reading, good company and reflection must finish him."

John Locke

Locke was an outspoken proponent for education being a stepping stone to greater things, not an end unto itself.

Here, he underscores the role of continuous self-improvement in shaping one's character and intellect. While formal education provides a foundation, true refinement comes from exposure to diverse perspectives, meaningful interactions, and introspective contemplation.

Think about the role of learning in your life. Remember that to reap its full benefits, it must be accompanied by continued curiosity, deep thought, and being around the right people to encourage you.

JULY 4

"Hope is a good breakfast, but it is a bad supper."

Francis Bacon

What a great line by Bacon, cautioning us against relying solely on optimism and wishful thinking without action.

Bacon acknowledges there is nothing wrong with hope, but it should be a starting point, not an ending point. Let hope serve as a source of motivation and inspiration, but then accompany it by deliberate effort and strategic planning to yield meaningful results.

An optimistic attitude, combined with concrete actions, is how big things get done.

JULY 5

"Live your life as an exclamation rather than an explanation. "

Sir Isaac Newton

Newton was good with the concise, pithy comment, wasn't he? Newton's exhortation to live life with passion and enthusiasm reflects a celebration of the human spirit and the pursuit of fulfillment and joy. He seems to be encouraging us to embrace opportunities and experiences with enthusiasm and zest, rather than getting bogged down by explanations and justifications.

Ask yourself if you are doing enough living, rather than simply conforming.

JULY 6

"Every man has his dignity. I'm willing to forget mine, but at my own discretion and not when someone else tells me to."

Denis Diderot

Diderot tended to explore the fine line of propriety and morality in thinking and behavior, a departure from some others of the time who were fixated on virtue.

His assertion highlights the importance of individual autonomy and self-respect. By asserting his right to define his own sense of dignity, he emphasizes the inherent value of personal agency and self-determination.

Perhaps true dignity arises from the ability to assert one's own identity and values, rather than conforming to external expectations or judgments, our imposing our standards on others.

JULY 7

"For every minute you are angry you lose sixty seconds of happiness."

Ralph Waldo Emerson

A humbling quote from Emerson, reminding us of the true cost of anger and bitterness.

Emerson's insight into the nature of anger and happiness reflects the broader philosophical themes of transcendentalism and the quest for inner peace and fulfillment. His emphasis on the fleeting nature of time and the preciousness of each moment resonated with individuals seeking to find meaning and purpose in their lives amidst the uncertainties of the 19th century. Emerson's message continues to resonate today, urging individuals to cultivate mindfulness and gratitude as they navigate the challenges of the modern world.

It is easier said than done, but try to minimize your time spent angry.

JULY 8

"There are three stages of scientific discovery: first people deny it is true; then they deny it is important; finally they credit the wrong person."

Alexander von Humboldt

Humboldt injects some humor into the discussion of the Scientific Revolution with this well-set-up line.

Humboldt's insight into the trajectory of scientific discovery reveals the challenges and resistance encountered by innovators throughout history. It is an important context for innovators, urging them to persevere in the face of adversity and remain steadfast in their pursuit of truth and discovery.

Not to mention, the fact that once the discovery is made, you might not end up with the credit you feel you deserve, but you will know you contributed to the truth.

JULY 9

"For heaven is within us, and people who have heaven within them come into heaven. The heaven within us is our acknowledgment of the Divine and our being led by the Divine."

Emmanuel Swedenborg

A recurring theme of Swedenborg's is trying to articulate heaven, and its relationship with the individual. In this line, he challenges us to recognize the divine spark that resides within each of us, urging us to cultivate a deeper connection to our inner selves and the divine presence that guides us.

Look within for the answers we seek, recognizing that the path to heaven—whether understood as a state of inner peace, fulfillment, or spiritual enlightenment—is found not in external pursuits or possessions, but in the depths of our own souls.

JULY 10

"No man, for any considerable period, can wear one face to himself and another to the multitude, without finally getting bewildered as to which may be the truth."

Nathaniel Hawthorne

Authenticity and integrity are critical in navigating the complexities of identity and self-expression. You can be more honest with yourself if you present as your true self to the outside world.

Hawthorne recognizes that it is human nature to sometimes filter your persona — to appear differently to the world than you do to your own conscience.

A person who presents different personas to themselves and others will inevitably lose sight of their true identity over time.

JULY 11

"I am more and more convinced that our happiness or unhappiness depends more on the way we meet the events of life than on the nature of those events themselves."

Alexander von Humboldt

This quote might remind some of the lessons from Victor Frankl's work, *Man's Search for Meaning*.

Humboldt's reflection on the nature of happiness and unhappiness speaks to the timeless quest for fulfillment and meaning in life, and as a reminder of the importance of perspective and attitude in shaping our experiences.

Humboldt seems to recognize the power of resilience and adaptability underscores the value of cultivating a positive mindset and embracing life's challenges as opportunities for growth and self-discovery. You will be dealt a hand of cards, but how you receive them and play them is completely up to you.

JULY 12

"How much of human life is lost in waiting."

Ralph Waldo Emerson

Emerson often writes about being in the moment, and not wishing time away. He seems to be doing that here, too.

If you are spending your time waiting for something or someone, you are letting time tick away without making the most of each moment. Emerson might suggest that instead of waiting, live for today. The thing you are waiting for will happen or not, whether you are making the most of this time or not.

Don't lose time waiting – it can be easy to do. Instead, be present and live for today.

JULY 13

"A truly virtuous man would come to the aid of the most distant stranger as quickly as to his own friend. If men were perfectly virtuous, they wouldn't have friends."

Charles de Montesquieu

Montesquieu's reflection on virtue and friendship proposes that perfect virtue would look past relationships and help others simply out of altruism and social bonds.

Montesquieu's words encourage individuals to reflect on the depth of their moral character and the sincerity of their relationships. By aspiring to embody the ideals of virtue and extending kindness not only to those close to us but also to strangers in need, individuals can foster a more inclusive and compassionate society.

Ask yourself if you are simply looking after your friends, or if you are being equally kind to all humans you come into contact with.

JULY 14

"To every action there is always opposed an equal reaction."

Sir Isaac Newton

Many of Newton's quotes have become timeless and immortal, and this is one.

Newton's third law of motion encapsulates a fundamental principle of the universe and serves as a reminder of the interconnectedness of all things. Newton's laws of motion provided a framework for understanding the physical world and laid the foundation for modern physics.

Outside physics, this quote reminds us of the importance of balance and equilibrium in all aspects of life, urging us to recognize the consequences of our actions. There will always be some, we just need to understand what they are.

JULY 15

"Nature can be so soothing to the tormented mind."

Alexander von Humboldt

Humboldt's observation on the healing power of nature reflects the Romantic ideals prevalent in the late 18th and early 19th centuries, a period marked by a renewed appreciation for the natural world and its restorative effects on the human spirit.

Humboldt's words served as a reminder of the therapeutic value of immersion in the natural environment. His emphasis on the calming influence of nature resonated with contemporaries seeking solace from the pressures of modern life, inspiring a renewed interest in nature and wilderness as sources of emotional and spiritual renewal.

⁻ This is true today, where some of the most successful people enter a period of celebrating nature after realizing the grind takes a toll on the mind.

JULY 16

"We should like to have some towering geniuses, to reveal us to ourselves in color and fire, but of course they would have to fit into the pattern of our society and be able to take orders from sound administrative types."

Joseph Priestley

Priestley gets into the Enlightenment Era spirit by taking a subtle dig at the administrative structures of the day.

His reflection examines the tension between individual creativity and institutional conformity. In Priestley's era, societal structures often prioritized stability and order over individual expression and innovation. However, Priestley suggests that the true value of genius lies not in its ability to conform to societal norms, but in its capacity to challenge and transcend them.

Are there things you want to do that are curtailed by our societal norms? Test the boundaries, and don't be afraid to be a little different.

JULY 17

"To succeed, jump as quickly at opportunities as you do at conclusions."

Benjamin Franklin

Franklin's humorous observation on seizing opportunities reflects his belief in the importance of decisiveness and agility in navigating life's opportunities and challenges.

It is human nature to jump quickly to conclusions, but Franklin says perhaps some of that bias-for-action should be reserved for taking action on things that matter and will actually create forward progress.

By embracing Franklin's advice to jump quickly at opportunities, individuals can position themselves for success and fulfillment in an ever-changing world.

JULY 18

"Plato is my friend, Aristotle is my friend, but my greatest friend is truth."

Sir Isaac Newton

Important context is that Newton lived 2,000 years after Plato and Socrates.

In this quote, Newton is paraphrasing a latin idea that you might find if reading about the early Western philosophers. Newton's allegiance to truth above all else reflects the Enlightenment emphasis on reason, empiricism, and the pursuit of knowledge.

His reference to Plato and Aristotle, two of the greatest philosophers of antiquity, underscores the importance of engaging with the ideas of the past while remaining open to new discoveries and insights. Newton's words remind us of the enduring value of truth as a guiding principle in the pursuit of knowledge and understanding, and that you can learn from those who went before you by reading.

JULY 19

"The expression of vanity and self-love becomes less offensive, when it retains something of simplicity and frankness."

Alexander von Humboldt

Humboldt's observation on vanity and self-love reflects his keen insight into human nature and social dynamics, a perspective shaped by the cultural and intellectual currents of the early 19th century.

His words served as a commentary on the complex interplay between our egos and the broader society.

Humboldt seems to be saying that it is Ok to admire and like yourself. But do so in a forthright matter-of-fact way. People will respect that more than the humble brag.

JULY 20

"What is success? To laugh often and much; to win the respect of intelligent people and the affection of children; to earn the appreciation of honest critics and endure the betrayal of false friends; to appreciate beauty; to find the best in others; to leave the world a bit better, whether by a healthy child, a garden patch, or a redeemed social condition; to know even one life has breathed easier because you have lived."

Ralph Waldo Emerson

Emerson, always focused on looking within, looks outward in this passage on how important the relationship with others and society is to a life well-lived. Noting the importance of personal fulfillment, meaningful relationships, and positive impact on the world, Emerson says true success is measured not by by the depth of our connections, the quality of our contributions, and the legacy of kindness and compassion we leave behind.

JULY 21

"An investment in knowledge always pays the best interest."

Benjamin Franklin

Franklin's wise words on the value of knowledge highlight his pragmatic approach to personal and professional development, a mindset reflective of the Enlightenment era in which he lived.

Franklin recognized the transformative power of education and lifelong learning. His emphasis on the long-term benefits of investing in knowledge resonates with modern readers, underscoring the importance of intellectual curiosity and continual self-improvement in achieving success and fulfillment.

Ask yourself, what will you learn today? If you can't answer the question, try to devote some time to building new knowledge of some sort, however small.

JULY 22

"Evil communication corrupts good manners. I hope to live to hear that good communication corrects bad manners."

Benjamin Banneker

Bannaker recognizes the transformative potential of communication, emphasizing its profound influence on human behavior and morality. He notes that what one chooses to say, and how they choose to say it, can negate otherwise positive temperament or behavior.

He also notes a hopeful aspiration for a reversal of this trend, articulating a desire to witness a future in which positive communication serves as a corrective force, fostering virtuous behavior and ethical conduct.

The lesson for us? It is not enough to act in the right way. Be sure that your words back it up. Be careful about what you say and how you say it, and about how it will be received by whoever you are communicating to.

JULY 23

"Well done is better than well said."

Benjamin Franklin

We see this theme recurring over and over among the Enlightenment thinkers. Perhaps they were disillusioned by centuries of leaders who did not live out their stated values.

This succinct aphorism captures Franklin's emphasis on action and practical accomplishment over mere rhetoric, reflecting his pragmatic outlook on life and work. Franklin's words served as a reminder of the importance of deeds over words in effecting meaningful change and progress.

His focus on tangible results and tangible achievements resonates with modern readers, highlighting the enduring value of hard work, perseverance, and diligence in achieving success and leaving a lasting impact.

JULY 24

"What we glean from travelers' vivid descriptions has a special charm; whatever is far off and suggestive excites our imagination; such pleasures tempt us far more than anything we may daily experience in the narrow circle of sedentary life."

Alexander von Humboldt

It was the Greek poet, Oved, who said "The grass is always greener on the other side." Nearly 2,000 years later, Humboldt expanded on the concept in his own words.

Humboldt's reflection on the allure of travel and exploration reveals his deep appreciation for the transformative power of firsthand experience and observation, a sentiment shaped by the spirit of scientific inquiry and exploration prevalent in the early 19th century.

At the same time, Humboldt is acknowledging the excitement in venturing beyond the confines of our daily routines, and being curious about the things around us every day.

JULY 25

"Human nature will not flourish, any more than a potato, if it be planted and replanted, for too long a series of generations, in the same worn-out soil."

Nathaniel Hawthorne

Nearly biblical in its tone and style, this Hawthorne analogy underscores the importance of diversity and renewal in sustaining the vitality and growth of human society.

Humans flourish when stretched. If one simply encounters sameness from day-to-day, year-to-year, and generation-to-generation, growth will be stifled.

Perhaps a practical, modern-day lesson Hawthorne would give us is to try new things, spend time with new people, read new books, and travel.

JULY 26

"It is a considerable point in all good legislation to determine exactly the credibility of witnesses and the proofs of a crime."

Cesare Beccaria

Beccaria's emphasis on the importance of credible evidence underscores the foundational principles of legal justice and fairness. Beccaria's wisdom serves as a reminder of the critical role played by evidence in the pursuit of truth.

While Beccaria might be writing for people in the legal or judicial professions, the concepts no doubt have lessons for all of us. When hearing about someone who has wronged another, ask yourself if the information is coming from a credible source. If not, believing or advancing the story may just serve as perpetuating a rumor. This can apply to interactions with society, in the workplace, or even in the role of parenting.

JULY 27

"It's not what you look at that matters, it's what you see."

Henry David Thoreau

The enlightenment thinkers placed a high value on an individual's intuition and self-trust. This Thoreau insight speaks to the power of perception and perspective in shaping our experience of the world.

This quote reminds us that we might all interpret different meanings from the same stimuli or experience. It encourages us to look beyond the surface and to cultivate a deeper understanding of ourselves and the world around us. True wisdom and insight come not from mere observation but from the ability to see beneath the surface, to discern the beauty and meaning that lies beneath. A curious, prepared mind will be ready to intake information with more meaning than someone simply going through the motions.

JULY 28

"Never ruin an apology with an excuse."

Benjamin Franklin

Franklin's astute line on the art of apology reflects his belief in the importance of sincerity and humility in repairing relationships and resolving conflicts.

So many of Franklin's best quotes are observations of human nature, and the tendency to make excuses when apologizing is universal.

Franklin's advice is to never ruin an apology with an excuse, individuals can cultivate healthier and more authentic relationships based on mutual respect and understanding.

JULY 29

"Our wants are various, and nobody has been found able to acquire even the necessaries without the aid of other people, and there is scarcely any Nation that has not stood in need of others."

Anders Chydenius

Chydenius was asked at times to help facilitate trade deals between various towns and regions, which undoubtedly aligned with the belief he writes about.

In this astute observation, he underscores the inherent interconnectedness of human society. He emphasizes that no individual or group can thrive in isolation and that cooperation and mutual aid are not just societal constructs but fundamental aspects of human nature.

By highlighting the natural inclination towards collaboration, Chydenius advocates for the promotion of policies and practices that foster mutual support and solidarity within and among nations.

JULY 30

"The heart wants what it wants - or else it does not care."

Emily Dickinson

Perhaps Dickinson's most famous line today, you will see references to it almost everywhere when you begin looking for it.

Dickinson's succinct observation speaks to the power of desire and longing in shaping our lives. It reinforces that the heart cannot always be reasoned with in a cerebral fashion – it has instincts that can't always be explained away.

The quote challenges us to listen to that voice inside us. It urges us to honor our deepest desires and passions, recognizing that true fulfillment arises from aligning our actions with our authentic selves.

JULY 31

"The more opportunities there are in a Society
for some persons to live upon the toil of others,
and the less those others may enjoy the fruits
of their work themselves, the more is diligence
killed, the former become insolent, the latter
despairing, and both negligent."

Anders Chydenius

Chydenius, always an economic thinker, keenly observes
the detrimental effects of societal inequality, where some
benefit at the expense of others. He argues that pervasive
exploitation erodes the work ethic of society, leading to apathy
and resentment among the exploited and entitlement among
the exploiters.

By highlighting the corrosive impact of inequality on
social cohesion and individual motivation, Chydenius advocates for policies that promote equity and fairness in the distribution of resources and opportunities.

AUGUST 1

"Every man is a volume if you know how to read him."

William Ellery Channing

Reminiscent of Kant's encouraging us to treat other individuals as an end rather than a means, Channing's metaphor underscores the complexity and depth of the human experience, inviting us to approach each individual with curiosity and empathy.

If we take time to genuinely get to know the people we encounter, we will not only have more success in our interactions with them, but we may find that they have stories and perspectives that are interesting and enriching.

This Channing line takes the adage "Don't judge a book by its cover" to a deeper level.

AUGUST 2

"Cherish those who seek the truth but beware of those who find it."

Voltaire

Voltaire has so many ideas that are perhaps more relevant today than when he wrote them, and this falls into that category.

Voltaire's admonition to "Cherish those who seek the truth but beware of those who find it" underscores the complexity of knowledge acquisition. In an era marked by philosophical and scientific enlightenment, where new ideas clashed with entrenched dogma, Voltaire's warning serves as a reminder to approach truth with humility and skepticism. He cautions against blind adherence to individuals claiming absolute truth, emphasizing the importance of critical thinking and intellectual independence in the pursuit of knowledge.

In short, value curiosity over certainty.

AUGUST 3

"A penny saved is a penny earned."

Benjamin Franklin

A quote often attributed to Franklin, but it likely existed before his time. Still, even if he paraphrased someone else, we will attribute it to him here.

The timeless aphorism on frugality and financial prudence reflects his practical approach to personal finance, a mindset shaped by the economic challenges of his time.

Wealth is not so much about what you make, it is about what you save. The more you can live below your means, the better off you will be. Building buying-power through saving is the same as earning more.

AUGUST 4

"Reading maketh a full man, conference a ready man, and writing an exact man."

Francis Bacon

In Bacon's reflection on the transformative power of reading, conversation, and writing, he illuminates the multifaceted nature of intellectual growth and self-improvement.

Bacon notes there are complementary roles of these activities in shaping the development of a well-rounded individual. Reading exposes one to diverse perspectives and knowledge, filling the mind with a wealth of ideas and insights. Engaging in meaningful conversation cultivates the ability to articulate thoughts and respond promptly to challenges, fostering adaptability and fluency of expression. Finally, writing refines one's capacity for precision and clarity.

Don't just rely on one channel in your learning and development. Read, discuss, and write, and you will find more clarity.

AUGUST 5

"Not I, nor anyone else can travel that road for you. You must travel it by yourself."

Walt Whitman

A line that almost evokes a coming-of-age feeling. There are certain things in life where you are the only one who can do it.

Whitman's assertion of individual responsibility for one's journey resonates from a standpoint of personal accountability and self-reliance. It is about empowering individuals to take charge of their own paths and decisions, and embrace autonomy and take ownership of one's life and choices.

It is a reminder that personal growth and fulfillment come from self-discovery and the willingness to navigate life's challenges independently.

AUGUST 6

"...Fatherland without freedom and merit is a large word with little meaning."

Anders Chydenius

Chydenius challenges the notion of patriotism divorced from the principles of freedom and meritocracy, asserting that true allegiance to one's homeland necessitates the presence of these foundational values.

Chydenius was, in fact, a vocal and influential advocate for freedom of the press, and his focus on individual freedom, and the ability to criticize authorities when warranted, are probably related.

He suggests that without freedom and merit as guiding principles, the concept of fatherland loses its significance, reduced to mere rhetoric devoid of substance. Through this assertion, Chydenius advocates for the cultivation of a society where liberty and merit are upheld as core tenets of national identity.

AUGUST 7

"Everything excellent is as difficult as it is rare."

Baruch Spinoza

A reminder that things that are truly excellent - be them experiences, items, or accomplishments - are so because they are rare or unique.

Spinoza's observation on the rarity and difficulty of excellence serves as a reminder of the value of perseverance and dedication in achieving greatness. Achieving a level of excellence requires resilience, refinement, and uncommon skill or mastery.

A growth mindset focuses on making yourself ever more rare, and striving for continuous improvement.

AUGUST 8

"Every man is guilty of all the good he did not do."

Voltaire

This statement, shrouded in a cloak of moral introspection, captures the essence of personal accountability and the weight of missed opportunities for kindness.

Voltaire, with his characteristic wit and insight, suggests that our failings extend beyond our actions to encompass the potential for positive deeds left unrealized. Through this lens, he challenges us to confront our own inertia and complacency, urging us to recognize the moral imperative of actively striving for goodness in all its forms.

Today, think about something that is suffering due to your inaction. Resolve to do something about it.

AUGUST 9

"We were together. I forget the rest."

Walt Whitman

How often have you heard someone say "When I'm talking to them, I feel like I'm the only person in the room"? Whitman's sentiment captures the essence of cherishing meaningful connections and experiences.

This Whitman line captures the importance of prioritizing relationships and shared moments over distractions or complexities. It is a call to treasure moments of genuine connection and to let go of unnecessary distractions in pursuit of deeper, more meaningful experiences.

AUGUST 10

"Life's tragedy is that we get old too soon and wise too late."

Benjamin Franklin

Franklin's poignant reflection on the passage of time and the nature of wisdom reflects his keen understanding of the human condition, a perspective shaped by his own experiences of aging and self-discovery. The words are a sobering reminder for modern readers to cherish the present moment and to seek wisdom and insight throughout the journey of life.

Franklin might also be suggesting that there is an important window of life when we still have some youthful energy, but are developing the wisdom that can only be created by time and experience. Take advantage of it.

AUGUST 11

"Observation more than books, experience rather than persons, are the prime educators."

Amos Alcott

Enlightenment thinking has always been about intaking information and the scientific method, rather than simply believing as facts everything you are told.

Keep in mind that Alcott was on a quest to change the educational system, and his emphasis on observation and experience as primary sources of learning underscores the importance of direct engagement with the world around us. Value the lessons that come from firsthand experience and personal reflection, and cultivate a spirit of curiosity and openness, embracing opportunities for exploration and discovery in our daily lives.

AUGUST 12

"No man chooses evil because it is evil; he only mistakes it for happiness, the good he seeks."

Mary Wollstonecraft Shelley

Motives are a complicated thing, and while we can't ever know what others are thinking, we can do a check on our own motives. Are you doing something in seeking happiness, that could in fact be a wayward path?

Wollstonecraft's insight into human nature reminds us of the complexity of moral decision-making. We are often driven by self-interest and short-term gratification, often with the consequence of wronging someone else. This quote challenges us to examine the underlying motivations behind our actions. Think to cultivate empathy, compassion, and moral integrity, recognizing that true happiness and fulfillment come not from selfish pursuits but from acts of kindness, justice, and virtue.

AUGUST 13

"The more often a stupidity is repeated, the more it gets the appearance of wisdom."

Voltaire

A quote that is so true today, in an age where a falsehood can be repeated, reshared, and read or watched millions of times within a day's time.

Voltaire's observation speaks to the enduring power of rhetoric and persuasion in shaping public perception.

Misinformation and propaganda can proliferate and gain legitimacy through repetition. Voltaire's insight serves as a reminder to exercise critical discernment and question prevailing narratives. His words underscore the importance of intellectual vigilance and independent thought in the face of manipulation and deceit.

AUGUST 14

"Thought is the sculptor who can create the person you want to be."

Henry David Thoreau

Many of Thoreau's most enduring lines have to do with intentionality, and this one is no different.

Thoreau's metaphor of thought as a sculptor underscores the creative potential of our minds in shaping our identities and destinies. The power we wield as architects of our own lives lies within our ideas and our consciousness. Thoreau challenges us to take ownership of our thoughts and beliefs, recognizing that they have the power to shape our perceptions, attitudes, and actions, and to cultivate a positive and purposeful mindset, sculpting ourselves into the person we aspire to become.

AUGUST 15

"Strive to make something of yourself, then strive to make the most of yourself."

Alexander Crummell

This quote emphasizes the importance of personal development and continuous improvement. It encourages individuals to not only establish themselves but also to push beyond their limits and maximize their potential.

By advocating for a relentless pursuit of self-betterment, Crummell underscores the idea that success is not merely achieved through initial accomplishments but through ongoing efforts to excel in all aspects of life.

Perhaps attaining your potential is a multi-stage process, and the first stage is to emerge as a productive member of society.

AUGUST 16

"People first feel things without noticing them, then notice them with inner distress and disturbance, and finally reflect on them with a clear mind."

Giambattista Vico

Vico often wrote about the human nature involved in reasoning and reflection, and this quote is a great example of that.

Vico's observation traces the predictable stages of understanding from visceral reaction to introspective reflection. His insight highlights the importance of mindfulness and self-awareness.

When you are trying to sort through a new concept, idea, or reality, don't fight it. Understand that you will likely go through stages of processing, and if you are lucky, you may end up with new knowledge.

AUGUST 17

"The great hope of society is in individual character."

William Ellery Channing

Societal change often seems daunting or overwhelming, like a big wave of groupthink and momentum taking over. This Channing quote challenges us to recognize the profound impact of individual actions and choices in shaping the collective destiny.

One could argue that the best societal improvement is made by every individual taking personal responsibility and accountability, recognizing that the future of society ultimately depends on the character and values of its individual members.

AUGUST 18

"The present is big with the future."

Gottfried Leibniz

Leibniz's aphorism encapsulates his philosophical concept of pre-established harmony, which speculates that the present moment contains within it the seeds of future possibilities.

Leibniz's insight offers a perspective of hope and anticipation for what lies ahead.

We think Leibniz is encouraging you and I to cultivate a forward-thinking mindset, embracing the potential for growth and transformation inherent in the present moment. By recognizing the interconnectedness of past, present, and future, individuals can approach life with optimism and resilience, navigating challenges with a sense of purpose and possibility.

AUGUST 19

"The only person you are destined to become is the person you decide to be."

Ralph Waldo Emerson

What a strong statement of free will. Emerson's words emphasize the importance of personal agency and choice in shaping our destinies.

In a society that often pressures us to conform to predefined paths or expectations, this quote reminds us that our future is not predetermined by external forces but rather by our own intentions, actions, and decisions. It urges us to take ownership of our lives and to strive towards becoming the best versions of ourselves. We have the ability to define our lives.

AUGUST 20

"We read the future by the past."

Alexander Crummell

This succinct statement encapsulates Crummell's belief in the significance of history as a guide for understanding and shaping the future. By recognizing the patterns and lessons of the past, individuals and societies can better anticipate the consequences of their actions and make informed decisions moving forward.

Crummell emphasizes the importance of learning from historical experiences, both triumphs, and failures, to navigate the complexities of the present and forge a path towards a brighter future. In essence, he underscores the timeless wisdom of studying history as a means of enlightenment and progress.

AUGUST 21

**"Words are the counters of wise men, and the
money of fools."**

Thomas Hobbes

Hobbes's observation underscores the importance of discernment and discretion in communication, and the fact that actions and words are ultimately the better judge of a human than their wealth.

The wise use words not merely as tools of communication but as vehicles for expressing profound insights and connecting with the universal truths that underpin existence. Conversely, "money" represents a shallow form of currency, symbolic of materialism and the pursuit of external validation.

As you navigate the world, be someone who is admired for your words (and character and reason) more than your wealth.

AUGUST 22

"If absolute sovereignty be not necessary in a state, how comes it to be so in a family? Or if in a family why not in a state? Since no reason alleg'd for the one that will not hold more strongly than the other..."

Mary Astell

Mary Astell's astute observation draws parallels between the tyranny of absolute power in the state and the patriarchal domination within the family structure.

Written at a time when male authority over women created countless cases of female subjugation, Astell outlines that families and households should be bound by the same basic freedoms that states are attempting to obtain.

This line is from the same passage where Astel questions "If all men are born free, how is it that women are born slaves?" quoted elsewhere in this book.

AUGUST 23

"Life is but a series of misunderstandings."

Denis Diderot

Reminiscent in tone to Newton's line, "I can calculate the motion of heavenly bodies, but not the madness of people," Diderot admires how hard it can be to understand others, and for them to understand you.

Given our human nature, nuance and misinterpretation are unavoidable aspects of living, underscoring the challenges of finding true harmony in social interactions.

Diderot's perspective encourages us to rely on humility and empathy, urging individuals to approach interactions with an awareness of the limitations of language and perception. One way he did this was through his famous "salons" where the exchange of ideas was the focus. They no doubt reinforced the effort involved in having different minds achieve a shared understanding.

AUGUST 24

"I have begun everything with the idea that I could succeed, and I never had much patience with the multitudes of people who are always ready to explain why one cannot succeed."

Booker T. Washington

Shift your thinking, so instead of asking "what could go wrong", ask "what could go right?" And if it does go right, what positive things will come of it?

This kind of optimism is something that we often see in Washington's writing. He seems to have a thread of positivity that is uplifting and forward looking.

Washington's attitude radiated resilience, inspiring hope and determination among those around him. Despite facing adversity, he maintained an unwavering optimism that fueled his tireless efforts towards educational empowerment and social progress.

AUGUST 25

"In all controversies, it is better to wait the decisions of time, which are slow and sure, than to take those of synods, which are often hasty and injudicious"

Joseph Priestley

How many times have you decided to "sleep on" a decision, and then return with a much clearer perspective of matters?

Priestley's insight into the nature of controversy challenges us to adopt a patient and deliberative approach to resolving conflicts. Priestly refers to the synods, which were church leaders assembled (sometimes hastily) to decide on pressing matters of rules or doctrines. Such synods would often get involved in the divisions and schisms within communities.

Priestley suggests that rash decisions made in the heat of the moment are unlikely to stand the test of time, but rather humility and restraint in the face of conflict will usually result in the most sound path forward.

AUGUST 26

"Either write something worth reading or do something worth writing."

Benjamin Franklin

Perhaps in our day and age of video streaming and social media, Franklin would modify this to "share something worth watching or do something worth sharing."

Franklin's pithy maxim on the importance of meaningful action and impactful communication embodies his belief in the power of words and deeds to shape the course of history. His emphasis on the importance of leaving a lasting legacy resonates with modern readers, reminding us of the enduring value of making meaningful contributions to society and leaving our mark on the world.

AUGUST 27

"Whether God exists or does not exist, He has come to rank among the most sublime and useless truths."

Denis Diderot

A common theme with many Enlightenment writers is their quest to try to reconcile a higher power with individual reason. Here, Diderot's contemplation on the existence of God challenges traditional religious beliefs and highlights the paradoxical nature of faith.

Diderot proposes that God could be both sublime and useless, and suggests that religious concepts can evoke awe and wonder while also remaining fundamentally unknowable and irrelevant to human existence.

Like many of his contemporaries, Diderot was skeptical towards organized religion, instead encouraging rational inquiry and critical thinking. While faith is always a personal choice, questioning dogma can be a useful exercise.

AUGUST 28

"To become truly great, one has to stand with people, not above them."

Montesquieu

Montesquieu was one of the main voices behind governments of the people, and of authority recognizing personal liberty. This line evokes that steadfast mindset.

The insight underscores the importance of humility and empathy in leadership. He noted that power often breeds arrogance and detachment – something that the Enlightenment thinkers so disliked about monarchies – and this quote challenges us to embrace a servant-leadership mindset. It urges us to prioritize the needs and concerns of others above our own ambitions, recognizing that true greatness lies in the ability to inspire and empower those around us.

AUGUST 29

"Simplify, simplify."

Henry David Thoreau

One of the short lines that Thoreau has become so known for, even in popular literature. The mantra serves as a timeless prescription for living a more meaningful and fulfilling life.

Probably more applicable today than when Thoreau penned it, this quote urges us to strip away the nonessential and focus on what truly matters. It challenges us to declutter our lives, both physically and mentally, and to embrace a simpler, more intentional way of living. Simplify one's life, create space for what truly brings joy and fulfillment, and live more deeply and authentically.

AUGUST 30

"There is nothing in the understanding which has not come from the senses, except the understanding itself, or the one who understands."

Gottfried Leibniz

Everything we know—our knowledge, our perceptions, our understanding—is rooted in what we experience through our senses. This is a theme we have seen with other Enlightenment thinkers, such as Locke and Vito.

Whether it's seeing, hearing, touching, tasting, or smelling, our senses are the gateway through which we interpret and make sense of the world. However, there's one crucial exception: the understanding itself, and the comprehension of it.

While our senses provide the raw material for our understanding, there's a deeper aspect of our consciousness—one that reminds us of the intricate interplay between perception, cognition, and the essence of our being.

AUGUST 31

"Oh! how near are genius and madness! Men imprison them and chain them, or raise statues to them."

Denis Diderot

Diderot's reflection on the relationship between genius and madness highlights the complex interplay between creativity and mental illness. By juxtaposing the confinement and idolization of genius, he suggests that society often struggles to understand and accommodate unconventional thinking and unconventional behavior.

We see this in the entrepreneurial and inventing world all the time. Someone who gets a little lucky is a hero. Someone else who did nearly the same things but didn't "hit" is considered a failure.

As you find inspiration for today, realize that while some might say you are crazy, you could actually be on the cusp of genius.

SEPTEMBER 1

"If all men are born free, how is it that all women are born slaves?"

Mary Astell

Written around 1700, when women were expected to tend to their husband's needs and have many children, Mary Astell's provocative question challenges the prevailing gender norms of her time.

The inequality and injustice experienced by women in society is well-documented. By juxtaposing the notion of universal freedom with the reality of female subjugation, Astell calls attention to the inherent contradiction between the principles of liberty and the social oppression of women.

We can ask ourselves, even today, "When we advocate for liberty, are we advocating for liberty for everyone?"

SEPTEMBER 2

"Man is an animal that makes bargains: no other animal does this – no dog exchanges bones with another."

Adam Smith

Smith's observation highlights the unique capacity of humans to engage in voluntary exchange and cooperation. The very mutual exchange that drives economic activity and social interaction is pretty unique to humans, at least when done for mutual benefit and not simply assisting out of evolutionary instinct.

Appreciate the ability of our species to cooperate in such a productive way. Smith seems to urge us to embrace the principles of reciprocity and mutual benefit, recognizing that voluntary exchange allows individuals to specialize, innovate, and create value for themselves and others.

SEPTEMBER 3

"By a lie, a man... annihilates his dignity as a man."

Immanuel Kant

Truth was so sacred to the Enlightenment thinkers, as it was to the Stoics before them. The next time you are tempted to lie, think about how that tears the fabric of your character.

Kant emphasizes the moral significance of truthfulness in this quote, suggesting that lying undermines one's dignity and moral integrity. He argues that deception erodes the fundamental respect and trust that form the basis of human relationships.

This quote reflects Kant's ethics, which prioritize honesty and integrity as moral imperatives. It reminds us of the importance of truthfulness in upholding our dignity and ethical principles.

SEPTEMBER 4

"If I can stop one heart from breaking, I shall not live in vain."

Emily Dickinson

Dickinson evokes so much human compassion and the profound impact of even the smallest acts of kindness with this line.

With a clarity of purpose that echoes through the ages, Dickinson articulates a universal aspiration—to alleviate suffering and bring solace to those in need. Her words resonate with a deep sense of empathy and altruism, challenging us to consider the legacy we leave behind and the measure of our lives not in personal achievements, but in the lives we touch and the hearts we mend.

Her words serve as a reminder of the transformative power of empathy and the enduring legacy of compassion. We can cultivate a spirit of generosity and kindness in our own lives, knowing that in doing so, we fulfill the highest purpose of our existence.

SEPTEMBER 5

"Color is nothing, anywhere. Civilized condition differences men, all over the globe."

Alexander Crummell

Crummell, a free black man living during the slave era, challenges the notion of racial superiority by asserting the inherent equality of all individuals regardless of race or ethnicity. He emphasizes that the significance of one's character and conduct far outweighs superficial distinctions such as skin color.

In a passage resembling what we later heard during the Civil Rights Movement, Crummel encourages us to overcome divisions based on race and ethnicity to foster genuine equality and unity among all people. This quote reflects Crummell's commitment to promoting racial justice and equality, advocating for a world where individuals are judged by their character rather than their skin color.

SEPTEMBER 6

"I went to the woods because I wished to live deliberately, to front only the essential facts of life, and see if I could not learn what it had to teach, and not, when I came to die, discover that I had not lived."

Henry David Thoreau

Self-reflection is paramount to the enlightenment thinkers and especially the transcendentalists. Thoreau's words epitomize the spirit of intentional living and self-discovery.

Thoreau teaches today's reader about the importance of slowing down, disconnecting from the noise of the world, and reconnecting with our inner selves. It evokes the "live an examined life" mantra, urging us to seek solitude and contemplation, to immerse ourselves in nature, and to reflect deeply on the true meaning of life. We can cultivate a deeper understanding of ourselves and our place in the world, enabling us to live more authentically and purposefully.

SEPTEMBER 7

"What speaks to the soul, escapes our measurements."

Alexander von Humboldt

How many times have you disagreed with someone, where one person was relying on data and the other on feeling?

Humboldt's reflection on the limitations of scientific measurement and observation reveals the humility and awe with which he approached the natural world. Humboldt's words served as a reminder of the inherent mystery and wonder of the universe, and the limitations of human perception and understanding underscored the importance of humility and reverence in the pursuit of knowledge.

The fact that there is still some mystery in the world, some intuition and feeling, is often comforting in an age when so much is reduced down to data and trends.

SEPTEMBER 8

"He that is good for making excuses is seldom good for anything else."

Benjamin Franklin

Ben Franklin was all about utility.

Franklin's blunt assessment of the futility of making excuses reflects his practical approach to personal responsibility and accountability, qualities that were highly esteemed in the 18th century. His emphasis on personal agency and self-reliance resonates with modern readers, underscoring the timeless importance of taking ownership of one's actions and choices in shaping one's destiny.

This quote applies to present-day life just as well. You are either someone who can get things done, or someone who can't. Try to be the former.

SEPTEMBER 9

"If God had not intended that Women shou'd use their Reason, He wou'd not have given them any, 'for He does nothing in vain."

Mary Astell

Advocating for women at a time when it was much more difficult for them to advocate for themselves, Mary Astell's assertion challenges the prevailing notion that women should be quiet and passive, and tend to the home.

By invoking the divine as the source of women's capacity for reason, Astell appeals to the believers of a higher power and undermines the traditional arguments used to justify women's subordination and exclusion from intellectual pursuits.

Astell's advocacy for women's education and empowerment was tireless. She was a trailblazing early feminist.

SEPTEMBER 10

"Today a reader, tomorrow a leader."

Margaret Fuller

A quote you may have seen in classrooms around the world.

Fuller's insight into the transformative power of reading underscores the importance of intellectual curiosity and life-long learning in cultivating leadership qualities. Embrace the habit of reading widely and voraciously, recognizing that the insights and perspectives gained from literature can inspire us to become influential leaders and changemakers in our communities and beyond.

You will be able to contribute more to society if you read than you will if you don't.

SEPTEMBER 11

"To be ignorant of one's ignorance is the malady of ignorance."

Amos Alcott

A quote you will see attributed to many, but to the best of our research it can be tied back to Amos Alcott – at least in the written form.

Alcott's insight underscores the importance of self-awareness and intellectual humility in the pursuit of knowledge. Certainty is often prized over curiosity, and changing one's mind can be perceived as lack of conviction. This quote challenges us to recognize the limits of our understanding and to remain open to new perspectives and ideas.

Start each day with an open mind. Embrace learning, curiosity, and understanding. There is a good chance it will make your day more interesting and fulfilling.

SEPTEMBER 12

"I apprehend you will embrace every opportunity, to eradicate that train of absurd and false ideas and opinions, which so generally prevails with respect to us."

Benjamin Banneker

Banneker's plea for the eradication of false stereotypes and misconceptions about African Americans reflects his commitment to truth and justice. By urging his audience to challenge ingrained prejudices and misconceptions, he advocates for a more enlightened and inclusive understanding of race and identity.

Banneker's words urge us to confront ignorance and prejudice with education and empathy, in order to foster greater harmony and understanding among all people.

SEPTEMBER 13

"The only fence against the world is a thorough knowledge of it."

John Locke

In this insightful observation, Locke emphasizes the importance of knowledge as a protective barrier against the uncertainties of the world.

Today, amidst a deluge of information and misinformation, Locke's words urge us to actively seek understanding and discernment. The more information flooding your attention, the more you need a solid foundation of knowledge and perspective to provide the right context for processing it.

By continuously seeking knowledge and broadening our perspectives, we can build mental resilience and shield ourselves from manipulation and ignorance.

SEPTEMBER 14

"There is no crueler tyranny than that which is perpetuated under the shield of law and in the name of justice."

Montesquieu

As much as he believed in their promise, Montesquieu spent lots of time thinking about what the pitfalls of a representative form of government could be. Here, his warning serves as a reminder of the dangers of authoritarianism disguised as legality.

Oppressive regimes often justify their actions through legalistic rhetoric or the appearance of doing the right thing, but this quote challenges us to remain vigilant against abuses of power and uphold the rule of law and to hold authorities accountable for their actions.

We can be on the lookout for the slippery slope. Is someone in power overreaching? Speak up, call them on it.

SEPTEMBER 15

"Every punishment which does not arise from absolute necessity, says the great Montesquieu, is tyrannical. A proposition which may be made more general thus: every act of authority of one man over another, for which there is not an absolute necessity, is tyrannical."

Cesare Beccaria

Beccaria's reflection on the necessity of punishment offers a critical perspective on the exercise of authority and the principles of justice. Beccaria invokes Montesquieu, who asserts that any punishment imposed without absolute necessity is tyrannical. This statement can be extended to suggest that any exercise of authority by one individual over another, without absolute necessity, is also tyrannical.

The words align with the Enlightenment sacred concept of personal liberty, and challenge us to ensure authority is exercised responsibly and with genuine need.

SEPTEMBER 16

"Guests, like fish, begin to smell after three days."

Benjamin Franklin

Franklin's wry observation on the perils of overstaying one's welcome reflects his practical approach to social etiquette and hospitality, a mindset shaped by the customs and norms of his time.

In the 18th century, social gatherings or family visits often lasted for days or even weeks, and Franklin's words served as a humorous reminder of the need for courtesy and consideration in hosting guests.

Set boundaries and maintain personal space – concepts that likely resonate with modern readers.

SEPTEMBER 17

"The most dangerous worldview is the world-view of those who have not viewed the world"

Alexander von Humboldt

Humboldt warns against the dangers of ignorance and narrow-mindedness reflects the broader cultural and intellectual currents of the early 19th century.

Written in an area of colonial expansion and cultural imperialism, Humboldt's words served as a critique of Eurocentric worldviews that sought to impose Western values and ideologies on diverse cultures and societies. His emphasis on the importance of direct experience and observation underscores the value of cultural exchange and cross-cultural understanding in fostering empathy and tolerance.

As you inject your ideas into the discourse of the day, work hard to gather as broad a perspective as possible. It will make your points and ideas stronger.

SEPTEMBER 18

"There is no excellent beauty that hath not some strangeness in the proportion."

Francis Bacon

Bacon observes the essence of true beauty, suggesting that excellence in aesthetics often emerges from a harmonious interplay of the familiar and the unconventional. He invites us to reconsider conventional notions of beauty and perfection and implies that true beauty transcends mere symmetry and conformity, finding its allure in the unexpected, the unique, and the unconventional.

In essence, Bacon suggests that it is the elements of strangeness and irregularity within an aesthetic composition that lend it a distinctive and captivating quality, evoking a sense of wonder and intrigue in the beholder.

Just being typical is not enough to stand out. The beautiful things have something captivating and unique about them.

SEPTEMBER 19

"If an historian were to relate truthfully all the crimes, weaknesses, and disorders of mankind, his readers would take his work for satire rather than for history."

Pierre Bayle

It has been said that truth is stranger than fiction, and Bayle seems to hint at that idea here.

Bayle's observation on human nature and historical truth sheds light on the complexities of interpreting the past. Humans are not entirely rational, and the stories of all the illogical things we have done could fill entire books.

Perhaps Bayle is suggesting that we should embrace history and the lessons we learn from it, but know that all of those people in the past were every bit as flawed as we are. Take the lessons and the teachings from them, but we may need to overlook all of the imperfections.

SEPTEMBER 20

"Doubt is an uncomfortable condition, but certainty is a ridiculous one."

Voltaire

Reminiscent of Marcus Aurelius reminding us to always ask ourselves if we might be the one who is wrong.

Voltaire's reflection on doubt and certainty highlights the limitations of dogmatism and closed-mindedness in the pursuit of truth. He seems to suggest that keeping some skepticism, even if the skepticism is aimed at your own conclusions, is important.

Like so many of the Enlightenment thinkers, Voltaire urges us to cultivate a spirit of humility and intellectual curiosity.

SEPTEMBER 21

"The less routine, the more life."

Amos Alcott

As a society, we have become consumed with routines, schedules, discipline, methods, procedures. Alcott doesn't think that is universally good.

Alcott's observation highlights the importance of spontaneity and novelty in living a rich and fulfilling life. In a world where routine and predictability often dominate our daily lives, Alcott challenges us to break free from the monotony of habit and routine.

One has to think the quote was inspired by Alcott's desire to make the child's classroom less rote and more free-flowing and spontaneous.

SEPTEMBER 22

"Fortitude is the guard and support of the other virtues."

John Locke

Locke recognizes the foundational role of courage in upholding moral principles and pursuing virtuous behavior.

In an era marked by rapid change and uncertainty, fortitude remains essential for navigating challenges and adversities with resilience. People can overcome obstacles and stay true to their values, even in the face of opposition or hardship.

Locke's insight serves as a timeless reminder of the importance of courage in fostering moral integrity and ethical leadership in both personal and professional lives.

SEPTEMBER 23

"While we maintain the unity of the human species, we at the same time repel the depressing assumption of superior and inferior races of men. There are nations more susceptible to cultivation, more highly civilized... but none in themselves nobler than others."

Alexander von Humboldt

Humboldt's advocacy for equality and human dignity reflects the ideals of the Enlightenment era, a period characterized by the pursuit of reason, liberty, and equality.

At the time of the writing, Humboldt was focused on the racial hierarchies he saw, and Humboldt's words challenged prevailing notions of racial superiority and inferiority.

His call for universal respect and recognition resonated with progressive thinkers of his time, and still serves as a reminder of the enduring importance of equality and human rights in the face of discrimination and injustice.

SEPTEMBER 24

"Difficulties are meant to rouse, not discourage. The human spirit is to grow strong by conflict."

William Ellery Channing

Along the same lines as a quote in this book from Amos Alcott, which is not surprising given that Channing and Alcott traveled in similar circles.

Channing's insight underscores the transformative power of adversity in fostering personal growth and resilience. Challenges and setbacks often provoke feelings of discouragement or defeat, but we can embrace difficulties as opportunities for self-discovery and development.

Confront obstacles with courage and perseverance, recognizing that adversity has the power to strengthen our character and fortify our resolve.

SEPTEMBER 25

"By failing to prepare, you are preparing to fail."

Benjamin Franklin

Franklin's pragmatic quip on the importance of preparation reflects his belief in the value of foresight and planning in achieving success, a mindset that he has become so well known for.

Today, Franklin's words serve as a timeless reminder of the importance of being proactive and taking responsibility for one's future. Modern readers can glean valuable insights from Franklin's emphasis on the necessity of preparation in navigating life's uncertainties and maximizing one's potential.

Preparing certainly doesn't guarantee success, but puts you in a state of mind where success will be more likely.

SEPTEMBER 26

"The straight line cannot proceed through the torturous twists of life."

Giambattista Vico

Perhaps Vico was drawing on his personal experience of chronic, recurring serious health issues when he wrote this line.

Vico's metaphorical statement resonates with the complexities and unpredictability of human existence. The importance of adaptability and resilience in the face of adversity is critical. By embracing flexibility and creativity, individuals can navigate the twists and turns of life with greater ease and effectiveness.

Many lives look like a nice, neat line when we zoom out. But upon closer inspection, we will often find that those same lives have had trials and challenges that we should strive to understand and appreciate.

SEPTEMBER 27

"Man is free at the moment he wishes to be."

Voltaire

A common theme throughout the Enlightenment Era is the reconciliation of free will with the determinism principles that had so dominated in the centuries leading up to it. This Voltaire line drives home that the power is within you to make your mind and your soul free.

It is a quote that reminds us of so many of the lessons from the iconic Victor Frankl work, *Man's Search for Meaning*.

As you go about your life, realize that while it might seem that the world is full of constraints, the power to be free is within you.

SEPTEMBER 28

"Everything good or true that the angels inspire in us is God's, so God is constantly talking to us. He talks very differently, though, to one person than to another."

Emmanuel Swedenborg

Enlightenment writers typically didn't pen heavily religious words, but Swedenborg was a notable exception. Swedenborg's notion is that divine guidance permeates every facet of our lives.

Regardless of religious beliefs, many of us find that a small voice of intuition and wisdom that speaks to us from within.

Swedenborg suggests that a bigger presence is persistent in our lives, guiding and directing us towards paths of goodness and truth. It invites us to open our hearts and minds to the divine messages that surround us.

SEPTEMBER 29

"Imagination is more robust in proportion as reasoning power is weak."

Giambattista Vico

Perhaps Vico was ahead of his time in realizing that there are left-brained and right-brained people, as is commonly suggested today.

Vico's provocative statement highlights the inverse relationship between imagination and analytical thinking. In today's data-driven society, where emphasis is often placed on logical reasoning and empirical evidence, Vico's insight offers perspective on the role of imagination in innovation and creativity.

We are at our best when we strike a balance between analytical rigor and imaginative exploration, embracing uncertainty and allowing room for creativity.

SEPTEMBER 30

"The special genius of women I believe to be electrical in movement, intuitive in function, spiritual in tendency."

Margaret Fuller

A colorfully descriptive assessment of how women are different.

Fuller's reflection on the unique qualities of women highlights the diverse and multifaceted nature of human potential. We can embrace diversity and uniqueness, recognizing that true progress and innovation arise from the intersection of different perspectives and experiences.

The quote was, no doubt, written at a time when nearly all prominent writers were male. Fuller's writing often advocates for society to appreciate the role and contributions of women.

OCTOBER 1

"The obligation of subjects to the sovereign is understood to last as long, and no longer, than the power lasteth by which he is able to protect them."

Thomas Hobbes

Hobbes clarifies that subjects are expected to obey the ruler or government only as long as the rule or government has the power to protect them.

Hobbes's reflection on the social contract underscores the reciprocal nature of political authority.

The quote from *Leviathan* underscores the fact that humans are first and foremost concerned about their own welfare. Hobbes' writing goes on to say that if a government or ruler is unable to protect them, it is logical for the individuals to take it upon themselves to do so.

OCTOBER 2

"Men will never be free until the last king is strangled with the entrails of the last priest."

Denis Diderot

A provocative statement from Diderot, and one that underscores the pervasive Enlightenment Era resentment of monarchy rules.

Diderot highlights the intertwined nature of political and religious oppression, and how linked individual liberty was to an "of the people" form of government.

Perhaps you are not on a mission to forcibly remove monarchs, but within your circle of control you have the power to dismantle oppressive structures and encourage the empowerment of the individual.

OCTOBER 3

I exist as I am, that is enough."

Walt Whitman

Born into a tumultuous era marked by rapid industrialization and social upheaval, Whitman emerged as a poet who celebrated individualism and embraced the complexities of human existence.

This quote, drawn from his seminal work *Song of Myself* in *Leaves of Grass*, epitomizes Whitman's rejection of societal norms and conventional constraints. It embodies an assertion of personal authenticity and self-worth, urging readers to embrace their unique identities without seeking external validation.

Perhaps, if he were here today, he would advise you to go through your day content that by being your authentic self, you are giving the world the best of you.

OCTOBER 4

"One truly understands only what one can create."

Giambattista Vico

John Locke said that "No man's knowledge here can go beyond his experience."

Here, Vico's provides a related but slightly different sentiment, that to gain true understanding, you must know the subject well enough to create from it. Both quotes focus on the important experiential aspect of learning.

Vico underscores the importance of active engagement and participation in the learning process, and encourages us to move beyond rote memorization and embrace a more dynamic and participatory approach to learning and understanding. Roll up your sleeves, get your hands dirty, and truly immerse yourself in the subject.

OCTOBER 5

"To be sane in a world of madmen is in itself madness."

Jean-Jacques Rousseau

Rousseau recognizes the challenges of maintaining one's sanity and moral compass in a world marked by chaos, noise, and confusion. Conforming to societal norms and expectations, which may be irrational or unjust, can feel like madness when surrounded by such circumstances. Rousseau speaks to the difficulty of preserving one's integrity and sense of purpose amidst prevailing madness and turmoil.

Looking at it another way, the quote also invites introspection and underscores the importance and responsibility of individual conscience and resilience in upholding principles of sanity and reason, to be ethical and pragmatic amid the chaos.

Don't be afraid to march to the beat of a different drummer. Yours may actually be the more reasoned beat.

OCTOBER 6

**"It is not the quantity but the quality of knowl-
edge which determines the mind's dignity."**

William Ellery Channing

Perhaps more important today, in an era of online references and artificial intelligence. Simply housing knowledge is
not as valuable as having critical ideas and unique
perspectives.

Channing underscores the importance of depth and
discernment in the pursuit of knowledge and understanding.

If you are able to, prioritize the quality of your learning
over mere accumulation of facts or data, and cultivate a spirit
of inquiry and critical thinking, recognizing that true knowledge arises from the depth of understanding and insight we
attain.

OCTOBER 7

"This is the best of all possible worlds."

Gottfried Leibniz

Leibniz's assertion, famously known as the "best of all possible worlds," encapsulates his philosophical optimism amidst the trials and tribulations of life.

Historical context is important here. Students of Leibniz believe he was stating that there is no reason that God – or a higher power – would create a world that was anything less than perfect. If a higher power created their best work anywhere, it would be here.

Voltaire, famously, satirized this later, as his more gloomy perspective noted that there are too many flaws and natural disasters for this to be someone's perfect work.

OCTOBER 8

"Every man is, no doubt, by nature, first and principally recommended to his own care; and as he is fitter to take care of himself than of any other person, it is fit and right that it should be so."

Adam Smith

Smith's reflection on self-interest underscores the importance of individual autonomy and self-reliance in the economy, but more broadly, in human affairs.

Personal responsibility can conflict with communal obligations, and Smith is defending an individual's instinct to put themself and their family first. Upon reading Smith's more broad work, one might make the argument that he believes if we each see to it that we are taken care of, the broader society will function more seamlessly for everyone. By helping yourself, you are better-equipped to help others.

OCTOBER 9

"It is dangerous to be right in matters where established men are wrong."

Voltaire

It is not just about being a contrarian, but it is also about who exactly holds hit predominant views that you are contrarian to.

Voltaire's cautionary observation underscores the risks of challenging conventional wisdom and authority. Conformity often stifles dissent and innovation, but questioning prevailing beliefs can be critical to progress.

Don't have the illusion, though, that questioning prevailing beliefs will be popular, and you just might find yourself going head-to-head with some pretty influential people.

OCTOBER 10

"Happiness is not found in things you possess, but in what you have the courage to release."

Nathaniel Hawthorne

Hawthorne urges us to remember that true happiness isn't measured by the possessions we accumulate, but by the intangible qualities we cultivate within ourselves.

It takes courage to let go of the material distractions and societal pressures that weigh us down. When we release attachments to what no longer serves us, we create space for personal growth, fulfillment, and deeper connections with others.

Embrace the liberating power of letting go, for it is through this act of courage that we discover the true essence of happiness and purpose in our lives.

OCTOBER 11

**"This view of a living nature where man is
nothing is both odd and sad. Here, in a fertile
land, in an eternal greenness, you search in
vain for traces of man; you feel you are carried
into a different world from the one you were
born into."**

Alexander von Humboldt

The notion of a natural world untouched by human presence may seem strange and even disheartening, but it also speaks to the enduring beauty and resilience of our planet.

In a landscape brimming with life and everlasting greenery, the absence of visible human influence offers a glimpse into a pristine realm untouched by the hands of man. While it may feel like stepping into an unfamiliar world, it serves as a reminder of nature's capacity for renewal and restoration.

This sentiment invites us to appreciate the majesty of the world around us and to consider our role as stewards of its precious resources.

OCTOBER 12

"A man is what he thinks about all day long."

Ralph Waldo Emerson

Emerson is channeling a strong free will philosophy with this line. It highlights the profound influence our thoughts have on our identity and behavior. It is a classic Transcendental Enlightenment way of thinking.

Much has been said about the importance of mindfulness and intentional focus. It challenges us to consider the quality of our thoughts and the impact they have on our attitudes, actions, and overall well-being. It urges us to cultivate a positive and purposeful mindset, directing our thoughts towards goals and aspirations that align with our values and aspirations.

OCTOBER 13

"Character, not circumstance, makes the person."

Booker T. Washington

Washington's insight encapsulates a timeless truth about personal development and resilience. In just a few words, he emphasizes the importance of character as the defining factor in shaping one's identity and destiny, transcending external circumstances.

This notion challenges the prevalent tendency to attribute success or failure solely to external factors beyond our control. Instead, Washington encourages individuals to focus on cultivating inner qualities such as integrity, perseverance, and determination.

Shifting the emphasis from external circumstances to internal character empowers individuals to take ownership of their actions and find inner fulfillment. Washington underscores the power of mindset and character in navigating life's journey with grace and purpose.

OCTOBER 14

"It is a sad reflection... that a sense of responsibility which comes with power is the rarest of things."

Alexander Crummell

Do you hold power, in your family, work, community, or an organization? With it comes a responsibility and duty.

Crummell's lament about the scarcity of responsibility among those in positions of power highlights the moral imperative of leadership. He observes that many individuals entrusted with authority fail to exercise it with the requisite sense of duty and accountability, leading to negative consequences for society at large.

If you have an opportunity to lead, practice ethical leadership. It will have a profound impact on the well-being of those you are leading.

OCTOBER 15

"Anyone can see that intending and not acting when we can is not really intending, and loving and not doing good when we can is not really loving."

Emmanuel Swedenborg

Actions speak louder than words. Swedenborg observes that if you had good intentions but made no impact, you might as well not even have had the intention.

The insight cuts to the core of human behavior, challenging us to align our intentions with our actions. True integrity lies in the congruence between our thoughts, words, and deeds.

As you approach the world, are you just providing lip service, or are you taking tangible steps towards making the world a little better for someone else?

OCTOBER 16

"He who hasn't tasted bitter things hasn't earned sweet things."

Gottfried Leibniz

Contrast is such an important part of life. We compare things, and make relative judgments, to decide what thing is better than another.

Leibniz's metaphorical statement underscores the value of adversity in shaping personal growth and resilience. We can embrace challenges as opportunities for learning and self-improvement, recognizing that setbacks pave the way for eventual triumph.

In today's world, perhaps this is a lesson in parenting. We so badly want to see our children succeed and be happy. But without some setbacks along the way, the accomplishments might not feel as satisfying.

OCTOBER 17

"It is not God's will merely that we should be happy, but that we should make ourselves happy."

Immanuel Kant

Kant often thought about the relationship between happiness and our existence, and this quote is another great example of it.

Here, he emphasizes personal agency and responsibility, suggesting that human happiness is not solely dependent on divine will but also on our own actions and choices. He challenges the idea of passive acceptance of fate or external forces determining our happiness.

Kant's emphasis on human autonomy and the importance of self-determination in achieving fulfillment and happiness is a common thread through much of his writing.

OCTOBER 18

"No testimony is sufficient to establish a miracle, unless the testimony be of such a kind, that its falsehood would be more miraculous than the fact which it endeavors to establish."

David Hume

This Hume passage about miracles is a powerful statement on the nature of evidence and skepticism. Hume's assertion highlights the need for rigorous scrutiny of extraordinary claims, and underscores the importance of applying critical thinking and logical reasoning when evaluating purported miracles or supernatural events.

Hume challenges us to question the reliability of testimonies and to weigh the probability of an event against the credibility of its witnesses.

Don't jump to conclusions based on correlative coincidences or one-off anecdotal stories.

OCTOBER 19

"Write it on your heart that every day is the best day in the year."

Ralph Waldo Emerson

If you need a pick-me-up, this line should help.

In true Emerson form, optimism is such an admired and important value. He encourages us to adopt a mindset of gratitude and positivity, recognizing the inherent value and beauty in each day.

We can easily be bombarded with distractions and negativity, this line serves as a powerful reminder to cultivate a sense of appreciation for the present moment and to approach each day with enthusiasm, curiosity, and a grateful heart.

OCTOBER 20

"The Bible is one of the greatest blessings bestowed by God on the children of men. It has God for its Author, salvation for its end, and truth without any mixture for its matter. It is all pure, all sincere; nothing too much; nothing wanting!"

John Locke

Locke's reverence for the Bible speaks to the enduring influence of religious faith on human culture and morality, something that Enlightenment thinkers were trying to reconcile with the newer scientific perspective.

While some may argue that parts of the bible provide detail that is lost on some readers, most scholars note that the writing style is succinct and efficient. Clearly, the bible has spoken to countless people over the centuries.

Whether it is the Bible or other sacred texts, know they can provide thoughtful perspective and anchoring to life principles.

OCTOBER 21

"No society can surely be flourishing and happy, of which the far greater part of the members are poor and miserable."

Adam Smith

Smith keeps a student of his on their toes – at times, he is steadfastly in the "every person for themself" camp, and other times he clearly thinks in terms of the broader societal social contract.

Smith's reflection on poverty and inequality highlights the social and moral implications of economic deprivation. Social disparities often lead to social unrest and injustice, this quote challenges us to address the root causes of poverty and inequality, and promote social mobility and economic opportunity for all members of society

True prosperity arises from the well-being and happiness of the entire community, not just a privileged few.

OCTOBER 22

"Uniform ideas originating among entire peoples unknown to each other must have a common ground of truth."

Giambattista Vico

A great observation by Vico that there seem to be some universal laws or truths, as evidenced by societies who have never interacted developing similar ideas and beliefs.

Vico's observation highlights the universality of certain truths that transcend cultural and geographical boundaries – a shared human experience.

It is a great reminder that if we approach people different from us with a high level of empathy, there is a very good chance we will find much that we have in common, even if our backgrounds could not be more different.

OCTOBER 23

"Love truth, but pardon error."

Voltaire

Voltaire's injunction to love truth while showing some grace for error underscores the importance of intellectual honesty and compassion in the pursuit of knowledge and understanding. Searching for truth and examining the way things are the way they are means we will sometimes get things wrong.

The safe route is to simply not challenge our beliefs or assumptions, to settle-in to a world where one is surrounded by their preconceptions and prejudices, something Voltaire also writes about elsewhere.

The better path is to ask questions, explore intellectually, knowing that you will not always get everything right.

OCTOBER 24

"Life is a journey, not a destination."

Ralph Waldo Emerson

Perhaps one of Emerson's most-repeated quotes, but one for which he is not often cited because it has become so commonplace. His words remind us to embrace the process of growth and discovery inherent in life's journey.

Still today, success is often equated with reaching a destination or achieving a specific outcome, this quote encourages us to savor the moments along the way, to appreciate the lessons learned, and to find joy in the ongoing pursuit of our aspirations. The experiences we accumulate, the relationships we cultivate, and the evolution of our person will ultimately define our life, not the final score or tally.

OCTOBER 25

"And thus, the actions of life often not allowing any delay, it is a truth very certain that, when it is not in our power to determine the most true opinions we ought to follow the most probable."

René Descartes

Descartes' contemplation on the uncertainty of life's circumstances and the necessity for action amidst such uncertainty speaks to decisions we are faced with on a daily basis. We would all love to be able to deliberate for as long as is needed, but in most situations that is not an option.

Descartes advocates for a pragmatic approach to navigating uncertainty—one that prioritizes practicality over perfection. Absolute certainty is unattainable, and a better approach is to think in probabilities.

OCTOBER 26

"Men for the sake of getting a living forget to live."

Margaret Fuller

You might recognize a famous Thoreau quote with many of the same words. Transcendentalists believed in experiencing life and not just going through the motions.

Fuller's observation highlights the tendency for individuals to prioritize conformity - often in the quest for material success - over personal fulfillment and well-being. This quote challenges us to reevaluate our priorities and values and to seek a balance between work and leisure, ensuring that our pursuit of a livelihood does not come at the expense of our happiness, relationships, and overall quality of life.

OCTOBER 27

"...as far as we are capable of knowledge we sin in neglecting to acquire it..."

Gottfried Leibniz

Leibniz's admonition the imperative that we all have to learn as much as we can, and understand as much about the world as is attainable to us.

It is a sobering reminder that our time on earth is short, and if we go about our years ignorant or aloof to new information, we may well have wasted some of our time and presence here.

As you go about your day, think "Is there more to this subject that I could seek to understand? What questions have I not asked?" Stay curious.

OCTOBER 28

"What is that you express in your eyes? It seems to me more than all the print I have read in my life."

Walt Whitman

Whitman's poetic observation about the expressive power of the eyes evokes the true essence of human connection and intuition.

So much of the Enlightenment is about the importance of empathy and intuition in understanding people and yourself.

This Whitman quote highlights the profound impact of non-verbal communication and the ability to discern meaning beyond words and recognizes the richness of human emotion conveyed through subtle cues like eye expressions.

OCTOBER 29

"A man's conscience and his judgment is the same thing; and as the judgment, so also the conscience, may be erroneous."

Thomas Hobbes

Hobbes observes that a person's conscience is intrinsically linked to their judgment. Just as our judgment can lead us astray, so too can our conscience be flawed. It is a sobering reminder that the moral compass within us is not infallible and can be influenced by erroneous reasoning — with dire consequences.

It is a reminder to be vigilant in examining and refining our judgments. History is replete with instances where even the most well-intentioned individuals have erred, led by a misguided conscience. It is through careful reflection and the pursuit of wisdom that we can strive to align our conscience with true and just principles.

OCTOBER 30

"A wise man will make more opportunities than he finds."

Francis Bacon

"You create your own luck" is something you have probably heard before. Bacon would likely agree with that assertion.

Bacon's reflection on the nature of opportunity notes that those who tend to be proactive and self-starting will find more opportunities in the world.

Some may immediately presume this quote is about professions and work, or about entrepreneurialism, and it sure can be. But you could apply the same proactive and activator mindset to your relationships, your community, or your intellectual or physical well-being.

OCTOBER 31

"Poetry must have something in it that is barbaric, vast and wild."

Denis Diderot

Diderot's description of poetry as "barbaric, vast and wild" challenges conventional notions of artistic expression.

By emphasizing the untamed and primal qualities of poetry, he suggests that true creativity defies convention and embraces the raw, unfiltered aspects of human experience. In Diderot's eyes, poetry pushes boundaries and explores new frontiers.

This quote reflects Diderot's appreciation for the transformative power of art, and his belief in the importance of artistic freedom and experimentation, urging poets to embrace the wild and unpredictable aspects of their craft.

NOVEMBER 1

"Perceptions which are at present insensible may grow some day: nothing is useless, and eternity provides great scope for change."

Gottfried Leibniz

A recurring theme in Leibniz writing was that new ideas take time to be proven, validated, and get traction. We see that time and time again in his work, and this quote is a perfect reflection of that.

Instant gratification often overshadows patience and perseverance when it comes to making new breakthroughs. Leibniz's insight offers a reminder of the value of patience and foresight.

Perhaps our takeaway from this quote is to be patient, be persistent, and eventually the most compelling and useful ideas will prevail. It just won't all happen at once.

NOVEMBER 2

"No matter how thin you slice it, there will always be two sides."

Baruch Spinoza

The idea that every question should be examined from multiple angles was an important breakthrough of the Enlightenment era.

Spinoza's line succinctly summarizes that having a duality in perspectives involves embracing complexity and nuance. No matter how much you dissect a topic, you will never stop uncovering counterpoints to your hypothesis or belief.

Empathy, open-mindedness, and the ability to see things from someone else's point of view are important aspects of reasoned thinking. Spinoza's wisdom encourages us to appreciate the richness of differing viewpoints and engage in constructive discourse that acknowledges the complexity of human experience.

NOVEMBER 3

"Solemnity is the shield of idiots."

Charles De Montesquieu

Montesquieu's blunt assessment of solemnity challenges conventional notions of seriousness and decorum. This is counter to some of the writing of other Enlightenment or earlier Stoic thinkers, and poses an interesting debate between the ideas. His words serve as a provocative reminder to question the authenticity and value of solemnity.

By encouraging individuals to embrace authenticity and spontaneity over keeping to oneself, Montesquieu's quote invites a reevaluation of the role of seriousness in human interaction and discourse. It prompts us to consider the merits of lightheartedness, gregariousness, and humor in fostering genuine connections and meaningful engagement with others.

NOVEMBER 4

"Common sense is the most widely shared commodity in the world, for every man is convinced that he is well supplied with it."

Rene Descartes

A humorous line from Descartes, observing the human nature of people to assume that surely they are not the ones who are in the wrong.

Descartes suggests that while common sense may be prevalent, it does not guarantee accuracy or reliability in one's perceptions or judgments. Instead, he implies the need for skepticism and introspection, encouraging individuals to question their assumptions and beliefs, even those considered common sense.

Keep yourself honest, and always ask yourself if you are as sure of your beliefs as should be. We can test our certainty and, in doing so, cultivate a deeper understanding of oneself and the world.

NOVEMBER 5

"No great discovery was ever made without a bold guess."

Sir Isaac Newton

Reinforcing the importance of a hypothesis in the scientific method, Newton's insight into the importance of boldness and creativity in the pursuit of discovery speaks to the element of exploration that is part of science.

His observation highlights the value of imagination and intuition in scientific inquiry, emphasizing the role of serendipity and inspiration in the process of discovery.

Perhaps, in our daily lives and work, we should be bolder. Put new ideas on the table, stick our neck out. The result might be that we generate an elevated level of curiosity and discovery.

NOVEMBER 6

"The mind, in proportion as it is cut off from free communication with nature, with revelation, with God, with itself, loses its life, just as the body droops when debarred from the air and the cheering light from heaven."

William Ellery Channing

One way in which the American reaction to the Age of Enlightenment contrasted with the 17th century European thinking was in its emphasis on communing with nature.

Here, Channing underscores the importance of connection with the natural world, spiritual truths, and inner self in nourishing the human spirit. Nature provides moments of solitude, reflection, and for some, connection with the divine.

Listen to the birds, feel the sun on your face. It is good for the soul.

NOVEMBER 7

"The end of knowledge is power."

Thomas Hobbes

Hobbes's insight into the relationship between knowledge and power underscores the transformative potential of understanding, and points to the profound connection between understanding and influence.

Knowledge is not merely a passive accumulation of facts, but a dynamic force that empowers individuals to shape their destinies and effect change in the world. True wisdom lies not in the possession of information alone, but in the transformative potential of applying that knowledge to achieve meaningful outcomes. In this sense, the pursuit of knowledge is not an end in itself, but a means to unlocking the latent power within each individual to inspire, innovate, and lead.

The quote reminds us a bit of the Thoreau line, "Be not simply good, be good for something."

NOVEMBER 8

"The sky is an enormous man."

Emmanuel Swedenborg

Swedenborg's metaphorical interpretation of the sky challenges us to expand our perception and embrace a broader understanding of the world around us.

Swedenborg's writing often tried to reconcile Christian beliefs with Enlightenment thinking, discussing the role of a person within the bigger picture. This line invites us to reconsider our relationship to the natural world and recognize the interconnectedness of all things.

Nature is perhaps not separate from us, but a reflection of our own inner landscape—a mirror that reflects the beauty, wonder, and mystery of the universe.

NOVEMBER 9

"Two things fill the mind with ever-increasing wonder and awe, the more often and the more intensely the mind of thought is drawn to them: the starry heavens above me and the moral law within me."

Immanuel Kant

Kant expresses a sense of wonder and reverence for two things in this quote: the vastness of the universe and the moral principles that guide human behavior. He suggests that contemplating the cosmos and reflecting on moral principles can evoke a sense of awe and fascination.

Kant's writing often shows his appreciation for both the natural world and the realm of morality, highlighting their significance in shaping human understanding and experience.

Perhaps we can use this inspiration to approach life with a sense of curiosity - both the vast world we live in and our thoughts and reason within us.

NOVEMBER 10

"We should let our godliness exhale like the odor of flowers. We should live for the good of our kind and strive for the salvation of the world."

Alexander Crummell

Crummell, a minister, was a philosopher but also someone actively working to spread the message of a higher power.

This quote reflects Crummell's call to embody virtues such as compassion, kindness, and altruism in one's actions. The imagery of godliness exhaling like the fragrance of flowers suggests that goodness should naturally emanate from within, enriching the lives of others.

Crummell underscores the importance of living with a sense of purpose and moral integrity, dedicating oneself to serving the greater good and working towards the betterment of humanity as a whole.

NOVEMBER 11

"Fetters of gold are still fetters, and the softest lining can never make them so easy as liberty."

Mary Astell

- Mary Astell

Astell is inviting us to consider the complex relationship between material comfort and personal freedom.

Imagine being adorned with golden chains—they might be shiny and luxurious, but they're still chains, binding you and restricting your movements. Astell suggests that no amount of comfort or opulence can compare to the intrinsic value of liberty.

Astell might urge us to prioritize autonomy and agency over mere material possessions, and remind us that true fulfillment comes from the ability to chart our own course in life, free from the constraints imposed by others or by society.

NOVEMBER 12

"No man's knowledge here can go beyond his experience."

John Locke

A thought-provoking quote that makes us question how much we really know.

Locke underscores the empirical basis of knowledge, emphasizing the importance of direct observation and personal experience. To truly understand the world around us, individuals must engage with reality firsthand, seeking out diverse experiences and perspectives.

At the same time, Locke seems to be reminding us that, no matter how smart we think we are, there is a whole world of information we don't have because of the limitations of our personal experience.

NOVEMBER 13

"Knowledge is power."

Francis Bacon

A quote you have undoubtedly seen, as it was later co-opted by President Thomas Jefferson.

Bacon's timeless insight resonates deeply for any one in a pursuit of enlightenment thinking and growth. Even more true in today's knowledge economy, those who possess valuable expertise and insights hold significant influence and control. Bacon's words go beyond policy or business. By having knowledge, you can have more power to design the life you want and live intentionally.

NOVEMBER 14

"Hope is the thing with feathers that perches in the soul."

Emily Dickinson

Dickinson was an optimist, and her writing often evoked positivity and hope. This line is no different.

The metaphorical depiction of hope as a resilient bird within the soul speaks to the enduring power of optimism and resilience. It is true that despair and uncertainty can often loom large, but this quote challenges us to nurture the flame of hope within us. It urges us to find strength and solace in the belief that brighter days lie ahead, even in the face of adversity.

Hope is always there, it can just take some effort to find at times.

NOVEMBER 15

"There is not less wit nor less invention in applying rightly a thought one finds in a book, than in being the first author of that thought."

Pierre Bayle

Bayle's reflection on creativity and innovation challenges conventional notions of originality, emphasizing the importance of intellectual synthesis and application.

We all learn from everyone who has gone before us. If we create a derivative thought inspired by someone else, Bayle is arguing it is perhaps as valuable as the original idea.

Interpretation and adaptation are essential skills, and are an important element of intellectual curiosity.

NOVEMBER 16

"He who is cruel to animals becomes hard also in his dealings with men. We can judge the heart of a man by his treatment of animals."

Immanuel Kant

Kant was always focused on trying to be a consistently good and humane person, and this idea takes that a step further.

Kant highlights the connection between how we treat animals and how we treat other people in this quote. He suggests that cruelty towards animals reflects a lack of empathy and compassion that can extend to human interactions as well.

This quote reflects Kant's belief in the importance of moral consistency and the interconnectedness of ethical behavior. It reminds us that our treatment of animals is a reflection of our character and moral values.

NOVEMBER 17

"Associate yourself with people of good quality, for it is better to be alone than in bad company."

Booker T. Washington

Washington emphasizes the importance of surrounding oneself with positive influences and supportive individuals.

How many times have you heard a reference to someone "falling in with the wrong crowd"? It can compromise one's ability to adopt health habits, have ambition, or even enjoy the basic elements of life.

One of the hardest things to do is to leave anyone behind, but think about the people you are surrounding yourself with. Do they bring happiness, encouragement, and fulfillment? If not, consider making adjustments.

NOVEMBER 18

"The natural effort of every individual to better his own condition ... is so powerful a principle, that it is alone, and without any assistance, not only capable of carrying on the society to wealth and prosperity, but of surmounting a hundred impertinent obstructions."

Adam Smith

Smith's observation on the power of self-interest underscores the resilience and dynamism of market economies. Many economic libertarian thinkers have relied on passages like this as they form their own thoughts, noting how political freedom is so often tied to economic freedom.

External forces can hinder economic progress, but this quote challenges us to recognize the self-regulating nature of free markets. The ingenuity and resourcefulness of individuals can overcome challenges and obstacles, and is superior to other approaches.

NOVEMBER 19

"New opinions are always suspected, and usually opposed, without any other reason but because they are not already common."

John Locke

Locke astutely observes the tendency of society to resist change and innovation merely due to its novelty.

The fact is that we all have inherent biases baked on our experience, societal norms, tradition, and habit. By embracing diversity of thought and being receptive to new ideas, we can foster innovation and progress in both personal and professional realms.

Your new ideas might be viewed with skepticism even if they have merit, and the ideas presented to you by others should be given a chance, even if they seem outside the box.

NOVEMBER 20

"A thing is not proved just because no one has ever questioned it."

Denis Diderot

Diderot was a skeptic, and this quote embodies that world view.

Simply because something has not been questioned does not make it inherently true or valid. True innovation and progress come from challenging the status quo and questioning assumptions. It's through this critical examination that we uncover new insights and possibilities, driving meaningful change and advancement.

Ask "why?" more often, about more things you encounter. There is a good chance that nobody else ever has.

NOVEMBER 21

"The Span of Life is too short to be trifled away in unconcerning and unprofitable Matters."

Mary Astell

Life is short, we hear that everywhere. Astell takes it a step further and instructs us to not waste time on things that have no utility.

Mary Astell's reflection underscores the preciousness of time and the importance of using it wisely and purposefully. The fleeting nature of life means we need to prioritize meaningful pursuits over trivial matters.

Astell challenges us to live with intention and purpose, and not let our days or years slip away from us wasting time on things that are not important.

NOVEMBER 22

"I know of no more encouraging fact than the unquestionable ability of man to elevate his life by a conscious endeavor."

Henry David Thoreau

One of Thoreau's most uplifting, optimistic lines. Resembling something Emerson might have written, Thoreau's words inspire us to recognize the power of personal agency and effort in shaping our destinies. In a world that often feels chaotic and unpredictable, this quote reminds us that we possess the capacity to transform our lives through conscious intention and action. It challenges us to take ownership of our circumstances, to set meaningful goals, and to pursue them with determination and perseverance.

By embracing the power of deliberate effort and intentionality, we unlock our potential for growth, success, and fulfillment, empowering ourselves to create the lives we desire.

NOVEMBER 23

"But it is not given to every electrician to die in so glorious a manner as the justly envied Richmann."

Joseph Priestley

Georg Richmann was an 18th century scientist who was killed by lightning while trying to study it.

Even today, scientific inquiry can be unpredictable or tragic. In Priestley's time, the pursuit of knowledge and discovery was fraught with danger and uncertainty, as evidenced by Richmann's fatal encounter with lightning. However, Priestley suggests that such risks are inherent to the pursuit of truth and enlightenment, and that those who dedicate themselves to experiment must be prepared to accept the consequences, however dire they may be.

It is a good reminder that in today's safety-focused world, sometimes one needs to take risks to make the biggest breakthroughs or advancements.

NOVEMBER 24

"Peace has in it trust in the Lord, that He governs all things, provides all things, and leads to a good end."

Emmanuel Swedenborg

While many enlightenment thinkers were trying to advance more secular and pagan thought, Swedenborg was always trying to reconcile reason with God. Here, Swedenborg suggests that true peace arises from a deep-seated trust in the divine order of the universe. It encourages us to relinquish our need for control and embrace the inherent goodness of life, recognizing that even amidst trials and tribulations, we are held in the loving embrace of a higher power.

Regardless of religious beliefs, this passage might prompt us to cultivate a sense of inner tranquility and resilience, knowing that no matter what challenges we may face, we are ultimately guided by a wisdom and love that is bigger than us.

NOVEMBER 25

"Crimes are more effectually prevented by the certainty than the severity of punishment"

Cesare Beccaria

Beccaria's insight into the efficacy of punishment offers a valuable lesson in the realm of criminal justice reform. We are more likely to obey rules if we know that punishment for ignoring them is guaranteed.

Beccaria's wisdom applies to how we think about negative consequences for actions that break rules. Even outside of the criminal field, enforcing rules consistently is key to them being taken seriously.

If you are in a position to apply laws or enforce rules or policies, see to it that there is a consistent consequence for now following them. That is more important than making the consequence severe.

NOVEMBER 26

"For me, my thoughts are my prostitutes."

Denis Diderot

A provocative statement from Diderot's *Le Neveu de Rameau* that illustrates his unconventional approach to intellectual pursuits. By likening his thoughts to prostitutes, Diderot suggests that we humans have the opportunity to flirt with whichever ideas we might have, however orthodox or appropriate.

This quote reflects Diderot's commitment to intellectual freedom and his willingness to push boundaries in pursuit of truth and knowledge. A powerful imagination is one of the benefits of being human, and we should not censor our thoughts, but rather keep a spirit of intellectual curiosity.

If you are to indulge, perhaps indulging in the creative realm of your thoughts is a great place to do it.

NOVEMBER 27

"Nature has established patterns originating in the return of events, but only for the most part. New illnesses flood the human race, so that no matter how many experiments you have done on corpses, you have not thereby imposed a limit on the nature of events so that in the future they could not vary."

Gottfried Leibniz

Leibniz's observation underscores the dynamic and unpredictable nature of natural phenomena, challenging deterministic views of the universe.

Looking backward, we can try to sort out and understand what has happened; that does not mean we will be able to accurately predict or anticipate what is going to occur in the future.

The fact that human existence is dynamic is one of the amazing things about it. Leibniz, in all of his writing, was effective at noting the mysterious element of life that will never go away, and that perhaps makes it so gratifying.

NOVEMBER 28

"If you want the present to be different from the past, study the past."

Baruch Spinoza

We have all heard the line, "Those who do not learn history are doomed to repeat it" which various derivatives have been attributed to many. Perhaps they all lean on this Spinoza idea.

Spinoza's insight into the transformative power of historical knowledge underscores the importance of learning from the lessons of the past.

We can cultivate a sense of historical consciousness and critically examine the events and decisions that have shaped the present. By studying the past, we can gain insight into patterns of behavior and societal dynamics, empowering them to make informed choices and shape a better future.

NOVEMBER 29

"I suppose therefore that all things I see are illusions; I believe that nothing has ever existed of everything my lying memory tells me... Perhaps only this one thing, that nothing at all is certain."

René Descartes

This passage is about skepticism, challenging the very foundation of Descrates' own perceptions and beliefs.

By expressing doubt about the reality of everything he sees and questioning the reliability of his own memory and senses, he embarks on a journey of self-examination.

If Descartes were talking to us today, he might encourage us to adopt a stance of critical inquiry and curiosity, urging us to question the assumptions and certainties that we often take for granted. The result may be new insights, perspectives, and truths that lie beyond the surface of our everyday perceptions.

NOVEMBER 30

"A moment's insight is sometimes worth a life's experience."

Oliver Wendell Holmes

A single moment of deep understanding can be more valuable than many years of living.

Sometimes, people spend their whole lives learning and experiencing things, but then they have one clear insight that changes everything. This one moment can give them more wisdom and clarity than all their previous experiences combined. It highlights the power of sudden realization and how it can shape a person's life in a significant way.

Consistency and habit is important, but don't neglect those flashes of understanding along the way. Welcome them.

DECEMBER 1

"Peace is not the absence of war, it is a virtue, a state of mind, a disposition of benevolence, confidence, justice."

Baruch Spinoza

Peace isn't just the absence of war, but something deeper. Spinoza describes it as a virtue, a mindset, and a way of behaving that's rooted in kindness, trust, and fairness. Spinoza suggests that true peace comes from within, from having a mindset of goodwill and fairness towards others.

The quote reminds us that peace isn't just about what happens on the surface, but about our attitudes and actions towards one another. It suggests that peace is a way of being, a way of thinking and acting that promotes harmony and understanding.

DECEMBER 2

"The end of law is not to abolish or restrain, but to preserve and enlarge freedom. For in all the states of created beings capable of law, where there is no law, there is no freedom."

John Locke

Laws are often seen as creating boundaries and constraints for how to behave. Locke has a different perspective.

Here, Locke elucidates that the fundamental role of law is actually in safeguarding individual liberties and allowing people to live free lives. Locke's perspective offers valuable insights into the delicate balance between freedom and regulation.

By upholding the rule of law and advocating for justice and equality, more people can achieve the freedom that humans deserve. It is a refreshingly positive spin on the idea of law and order.

DECEMBER 3

"Nothing is in the intellect that was not first in the senses, except the intellect itself."

Gottfried Leibniz

Leibniz's assertion underscores the sensory basis of human cognition, highlighting the role of perception in shaping intellectual understanding.

We should maintain a mindful awareness of our sensory inputs, actively engaging with the environment and honing our perceptual faculties. We can deepen their understanding and enrich our cognitive processes.

Leibniz's wisdom reminds us of the intrinsic connection between sensory perception and intellectual comprehension, guiding us towards a more holistic approach to knowledge acquisition.

DECEMBER 4

"Strip him of equipage and fortune, and such things as only dazzle our eyes and imaginations, but don't in any measure affect our reason or cause a reverence in our hearts, and the poor creature sinks beneath our notice, because not supported by real worth."

Mary Astell

Astell's observation critiques the superficiality of society's values and emphasizes the importance of inner virtue and moral integrity over material wealth and status.

By highlighting the transient nature of external adornments and the enduring significance of inner character, Astell challenges the prevailing emphasis on outward appearances and societal hierarchies.

This quote reflects Astell's belief in the inherent worth and dignity of every individual, irrespective of their social standing or financial position, underscoring her commitment to moral virtue and ethical integrity.

DECEMBER 5

"In the matters of religion, it is very hard to deceive a man, and very hard to undeceive him."

Pierre Bayle

Bayle observes that it is hard to change someone's opinion, especially if you are trying to convince them of something not so. But once they have bought-in to the falsehood, it can be just as hard to convince them of the truth.

Bayle's reflection on the enduring power of conviction and the challenges of challenging entrenched beliefs. It also speaks to the confirmation bias that each and every one of us is capable of holding.

The countermeasure, perhaps, is a spirit of open-mindedness and humility in our beliefs, and engaging in respectful dialogue and critical self-reflection.

DECEMBER 6

"The secret thoughts of a man run over all things, holy, profane, clean, obscene, grave, and light, without shame or blame."

Thomas Hobbes

Hobbes's reflection on the nature of human consciousness highlights the complexity and depth of the human psyche. It also shows that what goes on inside one's own mind are intensely private thoughts, and with this privacy comes a license to explore, imagine, and carry-on an internal dialogue and debate.

Inner turmoil often goes unnoticed, but this quote challenges us to acknowledge and confront our innermost thoughts and desires. It urges us to cultivate self-awareness and introspection.

Let your mind think and create. Don't constrain it. Just be sure that when it comes to words and actions, you have some control over it.

DECEMBER 7

"This I can declare: things that are in heaven are more real than things that are in the world."

Emmanuel Swedenborg

This line is classic Swedenborg, working to reconcile real-world life with the heavenly, spiritual life. He invites us to reconsider our understanding of reality and recognize the deeper truths that lie beyond the material world.

Swedenborg might be telling us that true fulfillment and meaning are found not in the pursuit of wealth or possessions, but in the pursuit of spiritual growth and enlightenment. It encourages us to look beyond the superficial trappings of modern life and cultivate a deeper connection to the eternal truths that lie at the heart of existence.

Those thoughts and ideas in your head, and the feelings deep in your soul, just might be more real than the things you own.

DECEMBER 8

"Virtue is a state of war, and to live in it we have always to combat with ourselves."

Jean-Jacques Rousseau

It is not easy to live a clean, virtuous life. In fact, some might say the path of least resistance would be to succumb to vices and evils.

Rousseau's reflection on the nature of virtue underscores the importance of self-discipline and moral courage in the pursuit of excellence. Living a good, kind life and striving for truth requires resilience.

While the Enlightenment thinkers were often careful to separate their religious beliefs from their philosophical ideas, this quote evokes sentiments from religions that recognize humans are flawed, that it is a victory to live each day as virtuously as possible.

DECEMBER 9

"Force and fraud are in war the two cardinal virtues."

Thomas Hobbes

Hobbes again gets a bit melancholy, as he characteristically does from time to time.

This quote is from a Hobbes essay on warfare, and this grim assessment highlights the brutality and deception inherent in conflict. It is an acknowledgement that in war, the concepts of right and wrong are no longer as applicable.

This quote challenges us to confront the harsh realities of human nature. It urges us to seek alternatives to violence and coercion, recognizing that true progress arises from diplomacy and negotiation rather than force and manipulation.

DECEMBER 10

"Do not weep. Do not wax indignant. Understand."

Baruch Spinoza

A succinct reminder from Spinoza that you have it within you to understand the things or people you are dealing with, by taking initiative instead of feeling the victim.

Spinoza's admonition to seek understanding rather than succumb to emotional reactions offers a profound lesson in emotional intelligence and resilience. Striving for understanding is the first step in overcoming adversity and finding inner peace.

You may be dealt challenges, but instead of letting them get you down, see them as opportunities for growth and learning.

DECEMBER 11

"The little flower that opens in the meadows lives and dies in a season; but what agencies have concentrated themselves to produce it! So the human soul lives in the midst of heavenly help."

Elizabeth Peabody

Peabody was an advocate for education and child development, and here she might be drawing a parallel between the many forces that help shape that child and the orchestra of things that come together to allow a flower to bloom.

It is an eloquent metaphor for the divine orchestration in growth and blossoming of life and knowledge. People thrive within a web of influences and guidance – ranging from person-to-person mentoring to divine and spiritual intervention – underscoring the interconnectedness of all creation and the presence of in every aspect of life.

DECEMBER 12

"In order that punishment should not be an act of violence perpetrated by one or many upon a private citizen, it is essential that it should be public, speedy, necessary, the minimum possible in the given circumstances, and determined by the law."

Cesare Beccaria

Beccaria spent lots of time thinking about crime and punishment, and this quote balances the importance of punishment with the fact that it can become violence in itself if used incorrectly.

Perhaps he was influenced by the tendency of monarchs to throw people in jail with little reason and for indefinite durations, and the idea that enlightened societies needed to be better than that.

Punishment should be swift, transparent, and the minimum possible, as Beccaria notes. Any more, and the punishment itself can be what perpetuates the violence.

DECEMBER 13

"To love truth for truth's sake is the principal part of human perfection in this world, and the seed-plot of all other virtues."

John Locke

In this powerful quote by John Locke, he suggests that valuing truth just because it's true is the most important thing for people to do. When we make truth our priority, it helps us become the best versions of ourselves and helps us grow other good qualities. Locke sees truthfulness as the foundation, like the soil where all the good qualities, or virtues, can grow from.

This line seems to emphasize the importance of uncovering the truth in order to truly understand a person's character and motivations. Admirable is Locke's belief in the centrality of truth to human perfection and virtue.

DECEMBER 14

"What wisdom can you find that is greater than kindness?"

Jean-Jacques Rousseau

Is there any virtue more profound or enlightening than kindness? The simple act of showing compassion and empathy towards others can illuminate our path forward.

Rousseau recognized that kindness transcends boundaries and divisions, fostering connection and understanding between individuals. It embodies a universal truth that resonates across cultures and generations—the transformative power of human decency and care.

As we celebrate other characteristics like strength, wisdom, clarity, and honesty, let's remember that kindness is not just a virtue but a towering guiding principle that can have a profound reach on everyone we interact with each day.

DECEMBER 15

"Early to bed and early to rise makes a man healthy, wealthy, and wise."

Benjamin Franklin

Franklin's famous adage on the virtues of early rising and healthy habits reflects his belief in the importance of self-discipline and self-care in achieving personal and professional success.

We see a resurgence in this concept today, with many of the health and wellness thinkers preaching the benefits of quality seem, consistent routines, and early wake-ups.

Anyone who has noticed how much more they get done in the early morning hours knows there is some truth to this quote.

DECEMBER 16

"Success waits patiently for anyone who has the determination and strength to seize it."

Booker T. Washington

This quote resonates with a timeless wisdom about the interplay between perseverance and achievement. In these few words, Washington elevates the importance of resilience and fortitude. Implicit in Washington's message is a challenge to the reader: "Are you willing to embody the determination and strength necessary to grasp the opportunities that await you?"

By framing success as a prize awaiting those with the courage, tenacity, and patience to claim it, he invites us to consider not only the external trappings of achievement but also the inner qualities of character and integrity that ultimately define our journey. Perhaps the true measure of success lies not in what we gain but in who we become along the way – an idea that repeats itself in Washington's writings.

DECEMBER 17

"The greatest minds are capable of the greatest vices as well as of the greatest virtues."

René Descartes

A common theme that we see in Descartes' writing is that intellect and mental capability can be used for both good and bad. It is as if he is warning his reader that it takes effort to apply our minds to good, and we should ensure we and those around us do.

We often idolize intellectual giants and public figures, this quote serves as a sobering reminder that greatness is not synonymous with moral virtue. In fact, the higher the mental abilities, the more that the person can do both good and harm.

Be sure you are using your IQ for constructive purposes, and recognize that those among us who are highly-intelligent have the capacity to be some of the most destructive.

DECEMBER 18

"If a man does not keep pace with his companions, perhaps it is because he hears a different drummer. Let him step to the music which he hears, however measured or far away."

Henry David Thoreau

A classic Thoreau passage with all the individualism we have come to expect from him. He celebrates the value of uniqueness and self-expression in a world that often pressures us to conform to societal norms or expectations.

The peer pressure to conform is every bit as strong today as it was back then, and this quote reminds us that true fulfillment comes from embracing our unique gifts, passions, and perspectives. It urges us to listen to the inner voice that guides us, to trust our instincts, and to march to the beat of our own drum, even if it means diverging from the crowd.

In short, live your own life.

DECEMBER 19

"Every person has a right to risk their own life for the preservation of it."

Jean-Jacques Rousseau

Rousseau's assertion of the individual's right to self-preservation underscores the inherent dignity and autonomy of every human being.

Rousseau's perspective remains relevant in affirming the importance of standing up for yourself, especially when the consequence might be an alteration of your "life, health, liberty, or possessions" as John Locke wrote at about the same time.

Risking life for being able to live with freedom is something that humans have done for centuries, and will probably continue to do until everyone can live with liberty.

DECEMBER 20

"An author is a fool who, not content with boring those he lives with, insists on boring future generations."

Charles de Montesquieu

Montesquieu's witty observation serves as a reminder to writers and creators about the importance of crafting meaningful and enduring work. If your message is not compelling in the here and now, why will it be compelling for posterity?

The quote underscores the responsibility of artists and authors to produce works that transcend the temporal and resonate with audiences across generations, urging creators to consider not only the immediate impact of their work but also its lasting legacy.

Be sure your work is engaging, relevant, and interesting for your society. If so, It will probably be admired by future generations too.

DECEMBER 21

"He that gives good advice, builds with one hand; he that gives good counsel and example, builds with both."

Francis Bacon

Bacon reminds us that the true architect of moral influence relies on both word and deed.

It is not enough to merely give guidance or advice; true leadership lies in the fusion of wise counsel with the living embodiment of action and virtue. Those who illuminate the path with both counsel and example will make a stronger impact on others, teach more effectively, and ultimately leave more of a legacy on the world.

Remember, as you go about your day, to lead with both advice and demonstration.

DECEMBER 22

"The despotism of many can only be corrected by the despotism of one; the cruelty of a single despot is proportioned, not to his might, but to the obstacles he encounters."

Cesar Beccaria

Beccaria suggests that the tyranny of a group of people can sometimes only be counteracted by the rule of a single leader, that the harshness of a single ruler isn't necessarily determined by their power alone, but by the resistance they face from others. Sometimes having one strong leader can be a way to bring order in a situation where many are acting unjustly.

Beccaria prompts us to consider how the actions of individuals and groups can influence governance and societal structures.

In turbulent times, be sure the leader speaking on behalf of the many is clear and powerful. This applies to organizations, communities, families – any social structure.

DECEMBER 23

"...every feeling is the perception of a truth..."

Gottfried Leibniz

Such an important line, and a great one to remember when you have that sense of an important emotion, idea, or feeling that you cannot explain.

Leibniz's proposition illuminates the profound relationship between emotion and cognition, suggesting that feelings serve as perceptual insights into underlying truths. Leibniz's insight offers a framework for understanding the significance of affective experience.

Don't discount that little voice inside of you. Listening to it can deepen your understanding and the world around you. Better yet, learn to put these feelings into clear words, and you just might become a great communicator.

DECEMBER 24

"We swallow greedily any lie that flatters us, but we sip only little by little at a truth we find bitter."

Denis Diderot

Diderot's words hit close to home in a day and age when so much information comes from the echo chambers of our choosing. It has never been easier to find sources that reinforce our biases, and Diderot's words might encourage us to seek out perspectives that are counter to our beliefs. You may change your mind, or you may at least gain an appreciation for the counter-argument.

The Diderot quote reminds us of a line from the 20th century musicians Simon and Garfunkle, "Still a man hears what he wants to hear and disregards the rest."

DECEMBER 25

"Let our posterity know that we, their ancestors, uncultured and unlearned, amid all trials and temptations, were men of integrity."

Alexander Crummell

How will your future lineage think about you?

The one thing we know is that they will know more than you do. Crummel acknowledges our descendents will probably have more intellect, but urges them to recognize the integrity of their forebears. If they know about our virtuous behavior, then we leave a legacy behind.

Integrity transcends time and circumstance, shaping the collective identity of a people and inspiring future generations to uphold the same principles of honesty, decency, and honor.

DECEMBER 26

"Act only according to that maxim whereby you can at the same time will that it should become a universal law."

Immanuel Kant

In this quote, Kant is talking about the importance of moral principles and universal rules, that when we make decisions, we should think about whether we would want everyone else to act the same way in similar situations. It asks the question, "Is this the right action assuming there are no conditions to it?"

This idea is called the Categorical Imperative, and it's a central part of Kant's moral philosophy. Kant believed that by following this principle, we can ensure our actions are morally right and fair.

This concept is a great test when you are faced with decisions and dilemmas, and can help provide clarity on what the right path or course of action might be.

DECEMBER 27

"The only way to have a friend is to be one."

Ralph Waldo Emerson

Emerson gives us a great reminder on how being a good friend doesn't need to be complicated.

In this timeless maxim, we are reminded of the reciprocity inherent in genuine relationships, a sentiment that resonates deeply with the principles of empathy and community that define the essence of friendship.

A friendship is a two-way street, made up of mutual respect, kindness, and shared understanding. Emerson urges us to draw on empathy to create bridges to the people around us.

DECEMBER 28

"Truth is ever to be found in simplicity, and not in the multiplicity and confusion of things."

Sir Isaac Newton

Newton's line is reminiscent of the ideas we see from others who were active during the rise of the scientific method. Sir Francis Bacon comes to mind.

Newton's advocacy for simplicity in the pursuit of truth reflects the Enlightenment ideal of rationality and clarity of thought. Newton's words serve as a reminder of the importance of critical thinking in distinguishing truth from falsehood.

His emphasis on simplicity echoes the sentiment of Occam's Razor, the principle that the simplest explanation is often the correct one. Don't settle for confusion, distill a question or a problem down to simplicity.

DECEMBER 29

"Act in such a way that you treat humanity, whether in your own person or in the person of any other, never merely as a means to an end, but always at the same time as an end."

Immanuel Kant

Perhaps one of Kant's more profound quotes, he argues that we should never use people as mere tools to achieve our own goals, but always respect their humanity and treat them with dignity and respect.

This idea is central to Kant's moral philosophy, known as the principle of humanity or the Formula of Humanity. Every individual has intrinsic value and should be treated as an end in themselves, rather than a means to someone else's ends.

With every interaction you have with others, know that they have their own story, experiences, and identity. Understand and appreciate who they are.

DECEMBER 30

"It is no use speaking in soft, gentle tones if everyone else is shouting."

Joseph Priestley

Some may disagree with Priestley's assertion that we need to dial-up our volume to match the moment, but there is some truth to it.

Priestley's reflection on the effectiveness of communication speaks to the importance of adapting our approach to suit the context and environment. In Priestley's time, public discourse was often characterized by impassioned rhetoric and fervent debate, where individuals sought to persuade and influence through forceful speech. However, Priestley suggests that in such a climate, soft-spokenness and gentleness may be ineffective in capturing attention and commanding authority.

It is useful to adapt our communication style to fit the demands of the situation. Speak with clarity, conviction, and the right force to match the situation and make an impact.

DECEMBER 31

"The more I read, the more I acquire, the more certain I am that I know nothing."

Voltaire

A fitting way final quote for the year. The more you learn, the smarter you become, the more humble you might find yourself.

How is it that the smartest, wisest people are so often some of the most humble? With wisdom comes a realization that the world cannot be reduced, and that getting your arms around the complexities of it can never be done.

Voltaire's reflection on the limits of knowledge highlights the openness required for genuine intellectual growth. Don't confuse cataloging information with truly understanding the world. The former can be done relatively easily in this day and age, but the latter is a lifelong question that can never end with absolute certainty.

Enlightenment Thinker Biographies

As we were compiling this book, we realized that for many, some of the thinkers quoted might not be familiar.

While the following biographies are brief summaries and not intended to replace other biographical works of the selected figures, you may find them to be an interesting companion to the quotes and lines in the book.

We listed them in order of birth year, rather than alphabetically. Why? Because we found that there is value in following how the Enlightenment and Age of Reason ideas proliferated from England and France, and then throughout Europe, and then across the ocean to America.

Listed in Order of Birth Year

Francis Bacon

Francis Bacon, born on January 22, 1561, in London, England, is the earliest thinker we profile and a towering figure of the Renaissance era. Raised in a family with connections to the royal court, Bacon received a comprehensive education in law, philosophy, and the humanities. He quickly rose through the ranks of the English aristocracy and held various positions in government, including as Lord Chancellor under King James I.

An enduring aspect of Bacon's life is his contributions to the scientific method, one of the key advancements that kicked-off the Enlightenment Era. In his seminal work, *Novum Organum*, published in 1620, Bacon outlined a new approach to scientific inquiry based on observation, experimentation, and empirical evidence. He emphasized the importance of systematically gathering data and testing hypotheses, laying the groundwork for modern scientific methodology.

Bacon's legacy extends beyond his contributions to science and philosophy. He was also a prolific writer and statesman, producing a wide range of essays, speeches, and literary works. Bacon's aphoristic style and keen insights into human nature earned him a reputation as one of the greatest English prose stylists of his time.

Bacon was a champion of reason, progress, and the pursuit of knowledge. His ideas on science, philosophy, and governance continue to influence thinkers and scholars across disciplines. Bacon's emphasis on the importance of empirical evidence and rational inquiry has left an indelible mark on Western thought and serves as a testament to his enduring legacy.

Thomas Hobbes

Thomas Hobbes, born on April 5, 1588, in Westport, England, was a renowned philosopher whose ideas profoundly influenced political theory and social contract theory. Raised during a time of political upheaval and civil unrest, Hobbes developed a pragmatic worldview that shaped his philosophical outlook. Despite facing adversity and experiencing the tumultuous events of the English Civil War, Hobbes' intellectual curiosity and keen intellect propelled him to prominence in the world of ideas.

In his famous work, *Leviathan*, published in 1651, Hobbes explored the nature of government, society, and human nature, arguing for the necessity of a strong central authority to maintain order and prevent chaos. His depiction of the social contract, in which individuals surrender some of their freedoms to a sovereign ruler in exchange for protection and security, remains one of the most influential concepts in political philosophy.

Hobbes' ideas on human nature and the role of government were controversial in his time and continue to provoke debate among scholars and thinkers to this day. His pessimistic view of human nature, characterized by the famous phrase "the life of man, solitary, poor, nasty, brutish, and short," challenged prevailing notions of human goodness and morality.

Despite his critics, Hobbes' ideas laid the groundwork for modern political theory and had a profound impact on subsequent philosophers such as John Locke and Jean-Jacques Rousseau.

Hobbes remained a tireless advocate for rational inquiry and the pursuit of knowledge. He made significant contributions not only to political philosophy but also to fields such as ethics, theology, and geometry. Hobbes' commitment to intellectual rigor and his willingness to challenge conventional wisdom continue to inspire scholars and thinkers to question assumptions and explore new ideas.

René Descartes

Descartes, born on March 31, 1596, in La Haye en Touraine, France, was a pioneering philosopher, mathematician, and scientist of the 17th century. Descartes grew up in a time of intellectual ferment, where he was exposed to various philosophical and scientific ideas. He received a Jesuit education, which provided him with a strong foundation in mathematics and classical philosophy.

Descartes' is known for his famous declaration, "Cogito, ergo sum," or "I think, therefore I am." In his seminal work, *Meditations on First Philosophy*, published in 1641, Descartes embarked on a quest for certainty and truth by subjecting all his beliefs to doubt. Through a process of radical skepticism, he arrived at the realization that the one thing he could not doubt was his own existence as a thinking being. This profound insight became the cornerstone of Descartes' philosophy and laid the groundwork for modern epistemology.

Descartes' contributions to mathematics were equally significant. He made groundbreaking advances in algebra and geometry, developing the Cartesian coordinate system that revolutionized the study of mathematics and laid the foundation for analytic geometry. Descartes' mathematical innovations not only transformed the field of mathematics but also had far-reaching implications for science and technology.

Descartes embodies the pursuit of knowledge and the search for truth. His dual legacy as a philosopher and mathematician continues to inspire scholars and thinkers to this day. Descartes' emphasis on rational inquiry and his insistence on the importance of doubt and skepticism in the quest for knowledge have left an indelible mark on Western philosophy and science.

John Locke

John Locke, born in England in 1632, was a philosopher whose ideas profoundly influenced the Enlightenment era. Growing up during a time of political and religious turmoil, Locke witnessed firsthand the consequences of authoritarian rule and religious intolerance. These experiences shaped his belief in the importance of individual liberty, reason, and tolerance.

Locke's impact on the Enlightenment can be seen in his writings, particularly his "Two Treatises of Government" published in 1689. In this work, Locke argued that governments should be based on the consent of the governed and that individuals possess natural rights to life, liberty, and property. His ideas challenged the divine right of kings and laid the foundation for modern democratic principles.

Locke spent time in exile in the Netherlands during the late 17th century, due to his criticism of those in power. Fleeing political persecution in England, Locke found refuge in the Dutch Republic, where he immersed himself in intellectual pursuits and engaged with other leading thinkers of the time. It was during this period that he developed many of his revolutionary ideas on government, human nature, and the social contract.

Locke's writings inspired revolutions and movements for

liberty around the world, including the American and French Revolutions. Locke's ideas continue to shape modern political thought and serve as a reminder of the enduring power of Enlightenment ideals in the quest for a more just and equitable society.

Baruch Spinoza

Baruch Spinoza might get our award for the "most underrated Enlightenment thinker." Spinoza's ideas were as revolutionary as they were controversial. Born into a Jewish community in Amsterdam in 1632, Spinoza's early years were marked by an intense pursuit of knowledge, leading him to delve into philosophy, theology, and science.

Despite his brilliance, his unorthodox beliefs soon brought him into conflict with religious authorities, eventually resulting in his excommunication from the Jewish community at the tender age of twenty-four. He spent years in relative solitude, focused on learning and writing.

Even with the ostracism and persecution, Spinoza remained steadfast in his commitment to reason and intellectual freedom, and his work influenced thinkers like Immanuel Kant and Albert Einstein. His emphasis on individual autonomy and the pursuit of truth continues to resonate in contemporary debates surrounding ethics, politics, and metaphysics. As one of the pioneers of the Enlightenment, Spinoza's legacy is one of critical inquiry and examination.

Sir Isaac Newton

Sir Isaac Newton, born on January 4, 1643, in Woolsthorpe, Lincolnshire, England, was a pioneering mathematician, physicist, and astronomer whose groundbreaking work laid the foundation for modern science. Newton grew up in rural England and displayed an early aptitude for mathematics and mechanics. Despite facing challenges and hardships in his youth, including the death of his father before his birth, Newton's intellect and determination propelled him to academic success.

Newton is known by many for his theory of universal gravitation. In his seminal work, *Philosophiæ Naturalis Principia Mathematica*, published in 1687, Newton introduced the concept of gravity as a force that governs the motion of celestial bodies. His theory of universal gravitation revolutionized our understanding of the universe and provided a mathematical framework for explaining the motion of planets, comets, and other celestial objects.

Newton's contributions to the field of mathematics were equally significant. He developed calculus independently of other mathematicians, laying the groundwork for the modern branch of mathematics. Newton's mathematical insights and analytical techniques continue to influence fields ranging from physics and engineering to economics and computer science.

Newton remained deeply curious about the natural world and dedicated himself to the pursuit of knowledge. His scientific achievements, including the laws of motion and the theory of gravity, have had a profound and lasting impact on human civilization. Newton's legacy as one of the greatest scientific minds in history continues to inspire generations of scholars, thinkers, and innovators.

Gottfried Leibniz

Gottfried Leibniz, born in Germany in 1646, was a polymath whose ideas left a lasting impact on the Enlightenment era. Leibniz developed a passion for knowledge and inquiry from a young age. He excelled in various fields, including mathematics, philosophy, and law, earning him a reputation as one of the most brilliant minds of his time.

Leibniz's contributions to philosophy and mathematics

were an important part of the Enlightenment Era. He developed the concept of calculus independently of Isaac Newton, laying the groundwork for modern calculus and mathematical analysis. Leibniz's philosophical writings, including his famous work "Monadology," explored complex ideas about the nature of reality, consciousness, and the universe.

Leibniz wanted to create international cooperation and understanding through diplomacy and intellectual exchange. He served as a diplomat for the Elector of Hanover, traveling throughout Europe to negotiate treaties and build alliances. Leibniz also corresponded with leading thinkers of his time, including Newton and the French philosopher Pierre Bayle, in an effort to foster dialogue and exchange of ideas.

Leibniz's impact was on an array of fields, including philosophy, mathematics, and computer science. Leibniz's emphasis on rational inquiry, intellectual curiosity, and the pursuit of knowledge remains a guiding principle in our quest to understand the world around us.

Pierre Bayle

Pierre Bayle, born in France in 1647, was a prominent philosopher whose ideas challenged traditional beliefs and paved the way for intellectual freedom. Growing up during a time of religious conflict and persecution, Bayle developed a deep skepticism towards dogma and authority. He believed in the importance of critical thinking and reasoned inquiry as the foundation for understanding the world.

Bayle's impact on the Enlightenment can be seen in his influential work, the *Historical and Critical Dictionary*, published in 1697. In this monumental work, Bayle examined a wide range of topics, including religion, philosophy, and politics, with a critical eye. He questioned established truths and argued for tolerance and intellectual freedom, laying the groundwork for the Enlightenment's emphasis on reason and skepticism.

Despite facing censorship and persecution for his controversial ideas, Bayle remained steadfast in his commitment to truth and reason. Like many Enlightenment activists, he spent much of his life in exile, moving from country to country to escape religious persecution and political turmoil. Despite these challenges, Bayle continued to write and publish his works, inspiring generations of thinkers with his fearless pursuit of knowledge.

Bayle's legacy is associated with religious tolerance, freedom of speech, and the separation of church and state. Bayle's commitment to truth and reason serves as a reminder of the importance of questioning authority and pursuing knowledge in the pursuit of a more just and enlightened society.

Mary Astell

Mary Astell, born in England in 1666, emerged as a notable figure in the Enlightenment era, advocating for women's rights and education during a time when such ideas were often overlooked. Growing up in a society that placed strict limitations on women's opportunities for education and intellectual development, Astell became a pioneering feminist philosopher and writer.

Astell's impact on the Enlightenment stemmed from her bold ideas challenging the prevailing social norms of her time. She argued passionately for women's right to education and intellectual freedom, believing that women were capable of the same intellectual achievements as men if given the opportunity. Astell's writings, including her influential work *A Serious Proposal to the Ladies* published in 1694, laid the groundwork for later feminist thinkers and helped pave the way for advancements in women's rights.

Astell helped create a charity school for girls in Chelsea, England, in 1709. Despite facing resistance from some members of society who opposed the idea of educating girls, Astell persisted in her efforts to provide educational opportunities for young women. The school became a beacon of hope for girls seeking to expand their horizons beyond the limited roles prescribed for them by society.

Astell's legacy as a pioneer of women's rights and education endures to this day. Her ideas challenged the patriarchal structures of her time and paved the way for progress in the fight for gender equality. Astell's contributions to the Enlightenment movement elevated the ideas of inclusivity and equality in the pursuit of knowledge and social justice.

Giambattista Vico

Giambattista Vico, born in Naples, Italy, in 1668, was a philosopher and historian whose writings helped Italy contribute to the European Enlightenment. Growing up, Vico developed a keen interest in understanding the nature of human society and history.

Vico's impact on the Enlightenment can be seen in his seminal work, *The New Science*, published in 1725. In this groundbreaking book, Vico proposed a radical theory of history, arguing that human societies follow cyclical patterns of development and decline. He emphasized the importance of studying human culture and institutions to gain insight into the laws that govern history.

Vico struggled to gain recognition for his ideas during his lifetime. Despite the originality and depth of his thinking, Vico faced opposition and indifference from many of his contemporaries. It was only in the centuries following his death that his contributions to philosophy and historiography began to receive the recognition they deserved.

Vico's ideas have proved timeless and have influenced

modern approaches to the study of history, culture, and society. Vico's emphasis on the importance of human creativity and imagination in shaping history remains relevant in our increasingly complex and interconnected world.

Emmanuel Swedenborg

Emmanuel Swedenborg, born on January 29, 1688, in Stockholm, Sweden, was a fascinating figure known for his diverse contributions to science, philosophy, and theology. Coming from a family of prominent scholars and nobility, Swedenborg received an excellent education in mathematics, science, and the humanities. His early career focused on scientific inquiry, where he made significant advancements in various fields, including engineering and anatomy.

Swedenborg's life was changed by his spiritual awakening and the subsequent shift in his focus from science to theology. In 1744, he claimed to have experienced a series of profound spiritual revelations that opened his eyes to the spiritual world. This transformative experience led Swedenborg to devote the latter part of his life to the exploration of theological concepts and the writing of religious texts.

Swedenborg's most notable work, *Heaven and Hell*, published in 1758, offered a detailed account of his visions and insights into the nature of the afterlife. He described heaven and hell as spiritual realms inhabited by souls after death, each governed by its own set of laws and principles. Swedenborg's writings on spirituality and the afterlife had a profound impact on religious thought and inspired the creation of the Swedenborgian Church, a denomination that continues to exist today.

Swedenborg was not just a theologian, he created a vast body of work that spanned multiple disciplines. His writings on theology, philosophy, and mysticism continue to fascinate scholars and spiritual seekers alike. Swedenborg's legacy as a visionary thinker and spiritual explorer endures, leaving a lasting imprint on the realms of religion, philosophy, and literature.

Montesquieu

Charles-Louis de Secondat, Baron de La Brède et de Montesquieu, known simply as Montesquieu, was born on January 18, 1689, in La Brède, France. A French philosopher and political thinker, Montesquieu rose to prominence during the Enlightenment era. He hailed from a noble family and received a thorough education in law, which would profoundly influence his later writings and ideas.

Montesquieu's groundbreaking work, *The Spirit of the Laws*, published in 1748, which explored the principles of political theory and comparative government, advocating for the separation of powers and the importance of checks and balances in maintaining liberty and preventing tyranny. His ideas profoundly influenced the framers of the United States Constitution and the structure of modern democratic governments.

Montesquieu's commitment to intellectual inquiry and the pursuit of knowledge extended beyond the realm of politics. He was also a pioneering scholar in the fields of anthropology and sociology, conducting extensive research into the customs, laws, and institutions of different societies around the world. His comparative approach to the study of human societies laid the groundwork for modern social science disciplines.

Throughout his life, Montesquieu remained a staunch advocate for individual freedom, constitutional government, and the rule of law. His ideas challenged prevailing notions of absolute monarchy and laid the foundation for modern democratic governance. Montesquieu's enduring legacy as a pioneering political thinker and advocate for liberty continues to shape political discourse and inspire movements for freedom and justice around the world.

Voltaire

You will see many Voltaire quotes in this book, in part because he was so quotable. His ability to distill ideas into a simple, hard-hitting line was special.

Voltaire, born François-Marie Arouet on November 21, 1694, in Paris, France, was a prominent French and Genevan figure of the Enlightenment era. Throughout his life, he became known for his sharp wit, prolific writings, and fierce advocacy for civil liberties and freedom of speech. Despite facing numerous obstacles and periods of exile due to his controversial views, Voltaire's impact on literature, philosophy, and politics was profound.

In his early years, Voltaire received a Jesuit education, but his rebellious spirit and questioning nature led him to pursue literature and writing. He quickly gained fame as a playwright, poet, and satirist, with works like *Candide* and *Letters Concerning the English Nation* earning him both acclaim and criticism. Voltaire's writings often targeted social injustices, religious intolerance, and abuses of power, earning him enemies among the clergy and ruling classes. At times, his criticism of those in power put his own life in danger, causing periods of exile.

Voltaire's legacy extends beyond his literary contributions. He was a staunch advocate for tolerance and reason, famously declaring, "I do not agree with what you have to say, but I'll defend to the death your right to say it." His ideas influenced thinkers across Europe and beyond, laying the groundwork for the principles of modern democracy and human rights. Voltaire's commitment to intellectual freedom and social justice continues to inspire generations to challenge authority, champion equality, and uphold the values of liberty and reason.

Today, Voltaire remains a highly-read and quoted thinker among academics, students, and readers.

Benjamin Franklin

Benjamin Franklin was a man of many talents and a key figure in American history. Born in 1706 in Boston, Massachusetts, he grew up in a large family and received limited formal education. However, he was a voracious reader and taught himself various subjects, including science and literature.

Franklin is, in fact, the earliest-born American thinker profiled in this book. He was a key part of bringing the new Enlightenment thinking to the new world, with his rare combination of intellect and energy.

Franklin became known in many fields, starting in business, and expanding to science, government, civic design, and others. He embraced the Enlightenment ideals of reason, scientific inquiry, and individual freedom. Franklin was not only a statesman and diplomat but also a prolific writer, scientist, and inventor. His experiments with electricity, including his famous kite experiment, helped advance scientific knowledge.

Franklin became known in his early career as a printer. As a young man, he ran away from his apprenticeship and journeyed to Philadelphia, where he eventually found work as a printer. To improve his writing skills, Franklin would read articles from the Spectator, a British publication, and then try to recreate them in his own words. This practice not only honed his writing abilities but also helped shape his own literary style.

Franklin founded libraries, fire departments, and educational institutions, leaving a lasting legacy as a founding father of the United States and a champion of the Enlightenment ideals of reason, liberty, and progress.

David Hume

David Hume, born on May 7, 1711, in Edinburgh, Scotland, left an indelible mark on philosophy and literature. Raised in a family of modest means, Hume showed academic promise from an early age. Despite financial constraints, he attended the University of Edinburgh, where he delved into the realms of philosophy and literature, shaping his intellectual trajectory.

Hume's seminal work, *A Treatise of Human Nature*, challenged prevailing notions of human understanding. Published in 1739, it posited that knowledge is grounded in sensory experience and cast doubt on the certainty of causal relationships. This skepticism laid the foundation for his empirical philosophy, which emphasized observation and evidence as the basis for knowledge.

An intriguing aspect of Hume's life lies in his time spent as a diplomat. In the mid-1730s, he served as an attache to the British embassy in Paris, where he immersed himself in French intellectual circles. This experience broadened his perspectives and provided insights that would later inform his philosophical and literary endeavors.

Throughout his lifetime, Hume produced a diverse body of work encompassing philosophy, history, and economics. His essays, including *An Enquiry Concerning Human Understanding*, delved into themes of morality, religion, and the nature of knowledge. Despite facing criticism for his controversial views, Hume's ideas endured, influencing generations of philosophers and leaving an enduring legacy in the annals of Western thought.

Jean-Jacques Rousseau

Jean-Jacques Rousseau, born on June 28, 1712, in Geneva, Switzerland, was a pivotal figure of the Enlightenment era.

Raised by his aunt and uncle after his mother's death, Rousseau's early life was marked by struggles and hardships. Despite limited formal education, he developed a deep passion for literature and philosophy, which would shape his influential ideas on politics, education, and human nature.

Rousseau's most famous work, *The Social Contract*, published in 1762, challenged conventional views on government and society. In it, he argued for the concept of popular sovereignty and the idea that governments should be based on the general will of the people. This revolutionary concept influenced democratic movements and political thought for centuries to come.

Rousseau's insistence on elevating the common good, which was a key part of his social contract, is perhaps one of the things he is best-known for. Much of his writing advocates for the rights of the weak or oppressed.

Despite facing controversy and persecution for his ideas, Rousseau's influence on Western thought was profound. His writings on education, including *Emile*, laid the groundwork for modern educational theory, emphasizing the importance of individualized learning and the development of moral character. Rousseau's ideas continue to resonate today, shaping debates on politics, education, and the nature of society.

Denis Diderot

Denis Diderot, a towering figure of the Enlightenment, revolutionized intellectual thought in 18th-century Europe through his pioneering contributions to philosophy, literature, and science.

Born in 1713 in Langres, France, Diderot's early education in Jesuit institutions instilled in him a thirst for knowledge and a critical spirit that would define his intellectual pursuits. His most enduring legacy is as the chief editor and driving force behind the monumental *Encyclopédie*, a comprehensive compendium of knowledge that sought to disseminate Enlightenment ideals to a wide audience. Diderot's impact on the Enlightenment era was profound. Diderot's own philosophical writings, such as *Pensées Philosophiques* (1746) and *Lettre sur les aveugles* (1749), reflected his commitment to humanism, empiricism, and the pursuit of truth through rational discourse.

Beyond his editorial endeavors, Diderot's plays and novels explored themes of moral ambiguity, existentialism, and the complexities of human nature. His writings challenged prevailing moral and religious norms, advocating for a more compassionate and empathetic society based on reason and free inquiry. Diderot's unwavering belief in the power of knowledge to transform society continues to resonate in modern discourse, inspiring generations of thinkers, writers, and activists to uphold the values of enlightenment and intellectual freedom.

Adam Smith

Adam Smith, born on June 16, 1723, in Kirkcaldy, Scotland, was a pioneering economist and philosopher of the Scottish Enlightenment. Growing up in a family of modest means, Smith demonstrated a voracious appetite for learning from an early age. He attended the University of Glasgow and later Balliol College, Oxford, where he studied moral philosophy and developed his intellectual interests.

Smith's most renowned work, *The Wealth of Nations*, published in 1776, laid the foundation for modern economics. In this groundbreaking book, Smith introduced key concepts such as the division of labor, the invisible hand, and the importance of free markets. His ideas revolutionized economic thought, advocating for minimal government intervention and emphasizing the role of self-interest in driving economic prosperity.

Smith had a close friendship with fellow philosopher David Hume (also featured in this book.) Despite their philosophical differences, Smith and Hume shared a deep mutual respect and admiration for each other's intellect. Their friendship endured throughout their lives, with Hume even assisting Smith in securing a teaching position at the University of Glasgow.

Throughout his lifetime, Smith made significant contributions not only to economics but also to moral philosophy and political theory. His ideas on capitalism, free markets, and the division of labor continue to shape economic policy and discourse to this day. Smith's enduring legacy as the father of modern economics underscores his profound influence on the course of human history.

Immanuel Kant

Immanuel Kant, born in Prussia in 1724, was a philosopher whose ideas had a profound impact on the Enlightenment era. Kant demonstrated a keen interest in questions about the nature of reality, knowledge, and morality. He believed in the power of reason and rationality to unlock the mysteries of the universe and guide human behavior.

Kant is known for many of his works, but his *Critique of Pure Reason*, published in 1781, is one that many associate him with. In this groundbreaking book, Kant sought to reconcile empiricism and rationalism by exploring the limits of human knowledge and the nature of experience. He argued that certain fundamental concepts, such as space, time, and causality, are inherent to the human mind and shape our understanding of the world.

On a personal level, Kant practiced a strict daily routine, which became legendary among his contemporaries. Kant was known for his punctuality and discipline, following a rigid schedule that included daily walks, meals, and study sessions. He believed that structure and routine were essential for intellectual productivity and self-improvement, and he adhered to his regimen faithfully throughout his life.

Kant had a profound impact on a wide range of disciplines, including philosophy, psychology, and ethics. Kant's emphasis on the importance of reason, autonomy, and moral duty remains a guiding principle in our quest to understand the world and live meaningful lives.

Anders Chydenius

Anders Chydenius, a figure less known but significant in the Enlightenment movement, was born in 1729 in Finland. He grew up in a time when Sweden ruled Finland, and despite the limited resources, he pursued education with fervor. Chydenius became a clergyman, economist, and politician, playing a vital role in shaping the ideals of the Enlightenment in his homeland.

Chydenius was a staunch advocate for individual freedom and economic liberty. He believed in the power of free markets and the importance of reducing government intervention in economic affairs. His writings, including *The National Gain* published in 1765, laid out his ideas on the benefits of free trade and the harmful effects of monopolies and excessive regulations. These ideas influenced not only Finnish society but also thinkers across Europe.

Chydenius spent time as a member of the Swedish parliament, where he fought against censorship and advocated for freedom of the press. In 1766, he delivered a passionate speech defending the right of ordinary citizens to criticize the government and express their opinions freely. This speech, known as the "Talpojkungen," or "The Peasant King," became legendary for its eloquence and courage in the face of oppression.

Chydenius's legacy as a champion of liberty and reason endures to this day. His ideas laid the groundwork for modern economics and democracy in Finland and beyond, making him a crucial figure in the Enlightenment movement and a symbol of courage and integrity.

Benjamin Banneker

Benjamin Banneker, born on November 9, 1731, in Baltimore County, Maryland, was a remarkable African American mathematician, astronomer, and inventor. Despite being born in a free state for African Americans, Banneker faced significant challenges due to racial discrimination and limited educational opportunities. However, his natural aptitude for mathematics and keen intellect allowed him to overcome these obstacles and make significant contributions to science and society.

Banneker played a role in the surveying and design of the nation's capital, Washington, D.C. In 1791, Banneker was appointed to the team led by Major Andrew Ellicott to survey the land for the new federal district. Despite facing racial prejudice and skepticism from some of his colleagues, Banneker's meticulous calculations and precise measurements played a crucial role in the layout and design of the city.

Banneker's most notable achievement came with the publication of his almanac. In 1792, he published "Benjamin Banneker's Almanac," which contained a wealth of information on astronomy, weather patterns, and agricultural advice. This almanac, which he continued to publish annually until 1797, not only served as a practical guide for farmers and astronomers but also showcased Banneker's intellect and erudition.

Bannaker's work helped elevate the thinking around social

justice and racial equality. He corresponded with prominent figures of his time, including Thomas Jefferson, challenging their views on race and slavery. Banneker's legacy as a self-taught mathematician, astronomer, and social reformer continues to inspire generations of African Americans and individuals around the world.

Joseph Priestley

Joseph Priestley, born on March 13, 1733, in Birstall, York-shire, England, was a polymath known for his contributions to science, theology, and political philosophy. Raised in a devout Calvinist family, Priestley showed an early aptitude for learning and pursued his education at Daventry Academy. He later became a dissenting minister, where he gained a reputation for his radical views on theology and politics.

An interesting fact is that Priestley discovered oxygen. In 1774, while conducting experiments on the properties of air, Priestley isolated a gas that he called "dephlogisticated air," which we now know as oxygen. His discovery revolutionized our understanding of chemistry and laid the foundation for modern theories of combustion and respiration.

Priestley's scientific achievements were matched by his prolific writings on theology and philosophy. He was a staunch advocate for religious toleration, social reform, and the rights of dissenters. Priestley's outspoken support for political and religious freedom made him a target of criticism and persecution, leading to his eventual emigration to the United States in 1794.

Priestley was about the pursuit of truth and the advancement of knowledge. His scientific discoveries, theological writings, and political activism left a lasting impact on the Enlightenment era and continue to inspire scholars and thinkers to this day. Priestley's legacy as a visionary scientist, theologian, and advocate for liberty endures as a testament to the power of intellect and conviction.

Cesar Beccaria

Cesare Beccaria, born in Italy in 1738, is a bit unique among the profiled thinkers in that he mainly wrote about one subject – crime and punishment. Still, his ideas on the subject made him a key Italian contributor to the Enlightenment movement, with his emphasis on criminology and legal reform. Particularly bothered by arbitrary and cruel punishments, Beccaria became passionate about advocating for justice and human rights. He believed in the power of reason and rationality to reform the legal system and ensure fairness for all individuals.

Beccaria's impact on the thinking around criminal justice can be seen in his influential work, *On Crimes and Punishments*, published in 1764. In this groundbreaking treatise, Beccaria argued against the use of torture and capital punishment, advocating instead for the principles of deterrence, proportionality, and the humane treatment of offenders. His ideas laid the foundation for modern criminal justice systems based on the rule of law and respect for human dignity.

Beccaria collaborated with other Enlightenment thinkers, including the philosopher Voltaire and the economist Adam Smith. Together, they exchanged ideas and corresponded on topics ranging from politics to philosophy to economics, contributing to the intellectual ferment of the Enlightenment era. Beccaria's ideas on legal reform and human rights resonated with his contemporaries and helped shape the course of Enlightenment thought.

Beccaria's contributions to the field of legal reform and criminal justice is what he is bet known for. His ideas continue to influence debates on criminal justice and punishment, inspiring efforts to promote fairness, equity, and compassion in legal systems around the world. Beccaria's commitment to reason, justice, and human dignity serves as a timeless reminder of the enduring power of Enlightenment ideals in the quest for a more just and enlightened society.

Mary Wollstonecroft Shelley

Mary Wollstonecraft exerted a profound influence on the intellectual and social landscape of her time through her advocacy for women's rights and her groundbreaking work on gender equality.

Best known for her seminal work "A Vindication of the Rights of Woman," published in 1792, Wollstonecraft challenged prevailing attitudes towards women's education and societal roles, arguing for their equal rights and opportunities. Through her writings, she laid the foundation for modern feminism, inspiring generations of activists and scholars to continue the fight for gender equality. Wollstonecraft's ideas on the importance of education, independence, and self-determination for women remain as relevant today as they were during her lifetime, serving as a beacon of enlightenment and progress in the ongoing struggle for gender justice.

Born in London in 1759, Wollstonecraft grew up in a household marked by financial instability and familial discord. Despite these challenges, Wollstonecraft displayed an early aptitude for learning and a fierce determination to carve out a path for herself. After working as a governess and a teacher, she turned to writing, publishing her first novel *Mary: A Fiction* in 1788. However, it was her groundbreaking treatise "A Vindication of the Rights of Woman" that would cement her reputation as one of the leading intellectuals of her time. Despite facing criticism and ridicule from her contemporaries, Wollstonecraft remained undeterred in her quest for equality, dedicating herself to the cause of women's rights with unwavering passion and conviction.

Wollstonecraft's tireless advocacy for women's rights – at a time when not many were speaking out – and her uncompromising commitment to equality continue to inspire feminists and activists around the world, serving as a rallying cry for those who strive to create a more just and equitable society. As we continue to confront the challenges of gender inequality and discrimination, Wollstonecraft's writings remain a source of inspiration and guidance, urging us to challenge the status quo and work towards a future where all individuals, regardless of gender, have the opportunity to thrive and fulfill their potential.

Alexander von Humboldt

Alexander von Humboldt, born on September 14, 1769, in Berlin, Prussia (now Germany), was a visionary explorer, naturalist, and scientist whose extensive travels and research reshaped our understanding of the natural world. Humboldt's early life was marked by a passion for learning and a thirst for adventure. Despite coming from a wealthy aristocratic family, he rejected a conventional career path and embarked on a journey of scientific exploration.

When he was 30, Humboldt went on a five-year expedition to South America from 1799 to 1804. Accompanied by French botanist Aimé Bonpland, Humboldt explored the diverse landscapes and ecosystems of the continent, documenting his observations in numerous journals and scientific publications. His expedition laid the foundation for modern biogeography and ecology and provided valuable insights into the interconnectedness of nature.

Humboldt's most enduring legacy lies in his holistic approach to scientific inquiry. He believed in the unity of nature and sought to understand the relationships between different elements of the natural world, from geology and botany to meteorology and anthropology. Humboldt's interdisciplinary approach to science foreshadowed later developments in fields such as ecology and environmental science.

Humboldt championed the importance of empirical observation and experimentation and promoted the dissemination of scientific knowledge to the broader public. Humboldt's writings and lectures inspired generations of scientists, writers, and artists, leaving an indelible mark on the fields of natural history and exploration.

William Ellery Channing

William Ellery Channing, emerged as a leading voice of American Unitarianism and a key figure in the intellectual currents of both the Enlightenment and Transcendentalist movements. Born in Newport, Rhode Island, in 1780, Channing was raised in a family deeply influenced by the principles of reason, tolerance, and religious freedom. His early exposure to the liberal Unitarian theology of his father, William Channing Sr., laid the foundation for his own intellectual and spiritual development.

Like James Freeman Clarke, Channing was himself a minister, as well as a lecturer, and writer. His influential sermons, including "Unitarian Christianity" and "Self-Culture," articulated a vision of religion grounded in reason, moral integrity, and the inherent dignity of the individual. Channing's emphasis on the power of reason and conscience in matters of faith challenged traditional Calvinist doctrines and paved the way for the emergence of Unitarianism as a distinct religious movement. His advocacy for religious tolerance and social reform reflected the ideals of the Enlightenment, promoting the principles of liberty, equality, and human rights.

William Ellery Channing's contributions to Transcendentalist thought are evident in his embrace of intuition, individualism, and spiritual self-discovery. His belief in the divinity of humanity and the potential for moral and intellectual growth resonated deeply with Transcendentalist thinkers such as Ralph Waldo Emerson and Henry David Thoreau who would come of age just a couple decades after Channing.. Channing's writings on the importance of personal experience and inner conviction in matters of faith foreshadowed the transcendentalist emphasis on intuition and the direct apprehension of truth.

Amos Alcott

Amos Bronson Alcott, a prominent figure of the 19th century and part of the famed Concord group, was not only an educator and philosopher but also a key contributor to the intellectual movements of Enlightenment and Transcendentalism. Born in 1799 in Connecticut, Alcott's early years were marked by a deep curiosity and thirst for knowledge. He embarked on a teaching career, deeply influenced by his belief in progressive education and the importance of moral development alongside intellectual growth. His own children were test subjects in this new way of educating, all of whom became high-achievers of the time including author Louisa May Alcott.

Alcott's writings often tie back to educational reform. As a fervent advocate for social reform and education, he founded the Temple School in Boston, which became a groundbreaking institution known for its innovative teaching methods and emphasis on moral philosophy. Alcott's belief in the inherent goodness of humanity and the power of education to foster individual growth aligned closely with the Enlightenment ideals of reason, liberty, and progress.

Amos Alcott's involvement in the Transcendentalist movement solidified his place in intellectual history. He was a close friend of Ralph Waldo Emerson and a member of the Transcendental Club, a group of writers and thinkers who explored ideas of intuition, individualism, and spiritual self-discovery. Alcott's writings, including his philosophical treatise "Orphic Sayings," reflected his Transcendentalist beliefs and his conviction that individuals could achieve higher states of consciousness through introspection and communion with nature. His influence on both educational reform and philosophical thought continues to be celebrated today, highlighting his enduring legacy as a pioneering thinker of his time.

Ralph Waldo Emerson

In a way, all roads from the Transcendental Enlightenment movement seem to lead to Ralph Waldo Emerson.

Emerson, born in 1803, was a towering figure of the Transcendentalist movement, best known for his essays, lectures, and poetry. Emerson championed individualism, self-reliance, and the pursuit of truth.

His seminal works, *Nature*, published in 1836, and the essay *Self-Reliance*, published in 1841, laid the foundation for Transcendentalism, a philosophical movement that emphasized the inherent goodness of humanity and the interconnectedness of all living beings. Through his writings, Emerson challenged traditional religious and societal norms, advocating for a more intuitive and spiritual approach to life.

Emerson's life was marked by a relentless quest for intellectual and spiritual enlightenment. He was raised in a Unitarian Boston household steeped in intellectual rigor and moral integrity. After graduating from Harvard College in 1821, Emerson embarked on a career in ministry, following in the footsteps of his father and grandfather. However, disillusioned by the dogma and conformity of organized religion, he eventually resigned from the ministry in 1832, setting out on a journey of self-discovery and intellectual exploration. He befriended several others featured in this book, a group from the Concord, Massachusetts area, including Henry David

Thoreau, William Ellery Channing, Margaret Fuller, Amos Alcott, and Nathaniel Hawthorne.

Emerson's literary career flourished in the years that followed, as he emerged as one of America's most influential writers and thinkers. His essays, including "Self-Reliance," "The American Scholar," and "Experience," captivated readers with their eloquence, insight, and moral clarity. Through his lectures and public speeches, Emerson inspired audiences across the United States with his impassioned calls for intellectual independence and spiritual liberation. A staunch advocate for social reform, he championed causes such as abolitionism and women's rights, using his platform to challenge the injustices of his time. Emerson's legacy endures as a beacon of enlightenment and inspiration, reminding us of the power of ideas to transform hearts and minds.

Nathaniel Hawthorne

Nathaniel Hawthorne, a master of psychological insight and allegorical storytelling, occupies a unique place in American literature, leaving an indelible mark on the Romantic era and beyond. Born in Salem, Massachusetts, in 1804, Hawthorne's upbringing in a town with a dark history of witch trials influenced his exploration of guilt, sin, and the complexities of human nature in his writing. His literary career took flight with the publication of "Twice-Told Tales" in 1837, a collection of short stories that showcased his skillful blending of moral ambiguity and supernatural elements.

Hawthorne's contribution to the Enlightenment era was multifaceted, marked by a deep fascination with the human psyche and the moral dilemmas inherent in societal norms. In works like *The Scarlet Letter* (1850), Hawthorne delved into the consequences of religious dogma and puritanical rigidity, challenging conventional notions of sin and redemption. Through characters like Hester Prynne, Hawthorne explored themes of individualism, self-reliance, and the quest for personal truth—a departure from the rigid conformity of his Puritan ancestors. His nuanced portrayals of human frailty and moral ambiguity resonate with Enlightenment ideals of rational inquiry and a rejection of blind faith.

Beyond his literary achievements, Hawthorne's impact on American letters lies in his enduring exploration of the human condition and the tensions between individual desires and societal expectations. Through his stories and novels, Hawthorne illuminated the complexities of human relationships and the perennial struggle for self-understanding. His introspective narratives laid the groundwork for the psychological realism that would define American literature in the 19th and 20th centuries. Nathaniel Hawthorne's legacy endures as a testament to the enduring relevance of Enlightenment principles—empirical observation, individualism, and moral inquiry—in shaping the trajectory of American literature and intellectual discourse.

Elizabeth Peabody

Elizabeth Peabody, born on May 16, 1804, in Billerica, Massachusetts, played a pivotal role in shaping education and literature in 19th-century America. Raised in a family of intellectuals and reformers, Peabody developed a deep passion for learning and social change from an early age. She became a prominent educator, author, and advocate for progressive causes, leaving a lasting impact on American culture.

Peabody's life is remembered by many for her pioneering work in early childhood education. In 1837, she opened the first English-language kindergarten in the United States, inspired by the educational principles of Friedrich Froebel. Peabody's kindergarten provided a nurturing environment for young children to learn through play and exploration, laying the groundwork for modern early childhood education practices.

Peabody's contributions to literature were equally significant. She played a key role in promoting the works of prominent writers such as Nathaniel Hawthorne, Ralph Waldo Emerson, and Henry David Thoreau through her bookstore and literary salon in Boston. Peabody's salon became a gathering place for leading intellectuals of the day, fostering dialogue and collaboration among writers, educators, and reformers.

Throughout her life, Peabody remained committed to advancing social reform and educational innovation. She advocated for women's rights, abolitionism, and the importance of education in shaping a democratic society. Peabody's legacy as a pioneering educator, influential literary figure, and champion of social justice continues to inspire educators, writers, and activists to this day.

James Freeman Clarke

Born in 1810 into a distinguished Boston family, Clarke was immersed from an early age in the intellectual fervor of the era. He attended Harvard College, where his inquisitive mind was shaped by the teachings of Unitarianism—a faith that emphasized reason and tolerance, a departure from the more orthodox doctrines prevalent at the time. Clarke's journey towards becoming a prominent minister and thinker began here, as he grappled with the intersection of religious faith and rational inquiry.

Clarke's life and influence were deeply intertwined with the broader currents of the Enlightenment. He spent considerable effort trying to reconcile Christianity with independent thinking, resulting in a need for theological reform. His writing and preaching were marked by a profound commitment to reason, moral progress, and social justice. Clarke's most enduring contribution was perhaps his emphasis on the inherent goodness of humanity and the belief in the potential for individual and collective improvement through education and ethical development. His ideas resonated deeply with his contemporaries, many of whom, however, were not religious. In this regard, Clarke added to the discourse of the time.

As a writer and theologian, Clarke wielded his pen as a potent instrument of change. His seminal work, *Ten Great Religions*, which explored the world's major faiths with an open and comparative perspective, encapsulated his belief in the universality of religious truths and the importance of tolerance. Clarke's legacy endures as a testament to the enduring power of reason, compassion, and intellectual curiosity in shaping a more enlightened and inclusive society. Through his life's work, he embodied the spirit of his age—a beacon of hope and reason amidst the tumultuous currents of the 19th century.

Margaret Fuller

Margaret Fuller, a remarkable figure of the 19th century, was not only a pioneering feminist but also a key contributor to the intellectual movements of Enlightenment and Transcendentalism.

Born in 1810 in Massachusetts, Fuller's early years were marked by a voracious appetite for learning and a passion for literature and philosophy. She pursued a rigorous education, immersing herself in the works of classical and contemporary writers, which laid the foundation for her later intellectual pursuits.

Fuller's contributions to the Enlightenment and Transcendentalism were profound and multifaceted. As one of the leading voices of the American Renaissance, she played a crucial role in shaping the intellectual landscape of her time. Fuller's groundbreaking work *Woman in the Nineteenth Century* challenged prevailing attitudes towards women's rights and gender roles, advocating for equality and autonomy for women in both the private and public spheres. Her ideas about individual freedom and social justice aligned closely with the Enlightenment principles of reason, liberty, and progress.

Margaret Fuller's involvement in the Transcendentalist movement solidified her place in intellectual history. She was a close associate of Ralph Waldo Emerson and a member of the Transcendental Club, a group of writers and thinkers who explored ideas of intuition, individualism, and spiritual self-discovery. Fuller's writings, including her influential essays and literary criticism, reflected her Transcendentalist beliefs and her conviction that individuals could achieve higher states of consciousness through introspection and connection with nature. She was a feminist trailblazer and intellectual luminary and continues to inspire generations of thinkers and activists, highlighting her enduring influence on both Enlightenment thought and Transcendentalist philosophy.

Henry David Thoreau

Henry David Thoreau, a leading thinker of the Transcendentalist movement, left his mark on the tail-end of the Enlightenment era with his profound philosophical insights and commitment to individualism and self-reliance. Best known for his literary masterpiece *Walden; or, Life in the Woods*, published in 1854, Thoreau championed a life of simplicity and contemplation in harmony with nature. Through his writings, he challenged the prevailing materialism and consumerism of his time, advocating for a return to the natural world as a source of spiritual renewal and moral awakening. Thoreau's influence extended far beyond his literary achievements, as he inspired generations of writers, environmentalists, and social activists with his reverence for the natural world and his uncompromising pursuit of truth and justice.

Thoreau held a steadfast commitment to his principles and beliefs. Born in 1817 in Concord, Massachusetts, he was raised in a family deeply rooted in the Transcendentalist philosophy. After graduating from Harvard College in 1837, Thoreau embarked on a career as a teacher, writer, and naturalist. However, it was his decision to live deliberately and deliberately in a small cabin beside Walden Pond in 1845 that would come to define his legacy. For two years, Thoreau immersed himself in the rhythms of nature, documenting his experiences and observations in *Walden* and laying the groundwork for his philosophy of simplicity, self-sufficiency, and spiritual communion with the natural world.

Thoreau's legacy endures as a beacon of enlightenment and inspiration, reminding us of the power of the individual to effect change and shape the course of history. His writings on civil disobedience and nonviolent resistance would later influence leaders such as Mahatma Gandhi and Martin Luther King Jr., who cited Thoreau as a source of inspiration in their struggles for social justice and human rights. Thoreau's commitment to living authentically and ethically in harmony with nature continues to resonate with readers around the world, serving as a timeless reminder of the enduring importance of integrity, resilience, and moral courage in the face of adversity.

Walt Whitman

You can often identify a Walt Whitman quote by how succinct and rich it is at the same time. Often hailed as the "Bard of Democracy," Whitman left his mark on American literature and culture, with a spirit of individualism and enlightenment ideals during a pivotal era in history.

Born in 1819 on Long Island, New York, Whitman came

of age during a time of rapid industrialization and social change. His poetic journey began with an insatiable curiosity about the human experience and an ardent belief in the inherent dignity and worth of every individual. Whitman's groundbreaking work, *Leaves of Grass*, published in 1855, challenged conventional literary norms and ushered in a new era of poetic expression characterized by free verse and candid exploration of universal themes.

Whitman's contribution to the Enlightenment era was profound, as he championed the principles of reason, individualism, and egalitarianism through his poetry. In *Leaves of Grass*, Whitman celebrated the diversity of human existence and embraced the interconnectedness of all living beings, emphasizing the importance of self-discovery and personal authenticity. His poems, such as *Song of Myself*, exuded a sense of democratic optimism and a belief in the inherent goodness of humanity. Whitman's celebration of the physical body and the natural world reflected Enlightenment ideals of humanism and the pursuit of knowledge grounded in empirical observation.

During the Civil War, his poems took on a patriotic fervor, expressing a vision of national unity and the struggle for justice and equality. His unwavering commitment to the principles of enlightenment—truth, liberty, and progress—continues to inspire generations of poets, thinkers, and activists striving to create a more just and enlightened society.

Alexander Crummell

Alexander Crummell, born in New York City in 1819, was a pioneering African-American intellectual and religious leader. Growing up in a time of slavery and racial oppression, Crummell faced many obstacles to his education and advancement. However, he persevered, becoming one of the leading voices of the African-American community in the 19th century.

Crummell was deeply influenced by the Enlightenment ideals of reason, education, and equality. He believed fervently in the power of education to uplift individuals and communities, advocating for the importance of intellectual development among African Americans. Crummell himself pursued a rigorous education, studying at institutions such as Queens College in Cambridge, Massachusetts, and the University of Oxford in England.

Crummell is known by many for his effort to establish schools and institutions for the education of African Americans. Despite facing resistance and discrimination, he founded the American Negro Academy in 1897, an organization dedicated to promoting scholarship and intellectual achievement among African Americans. Crummell's vision laid the groundwork for the civil rights movement and the pursuit of equality in America.

Crummell's impact on the Enlightenment was profound, as he sought to apply its principles of reason and equality to the struggle for racial justice. Through his writings, speeches, and advocacy, he inspired generations of African Americans to pursue education, self-improvement, and social progress. Crummell's legacy continues to resonate today, reminding us of the enduring power of ideas in the fight for freedom and equality.

Emily Dickinson

Emily Dickinson's ability to be powerful yet efficient with words is recognizable even to the casual reader.

Emily Dickinson, born on December 10, 1830, in Amherst, Massachusetts, is widely regarded as one of America's greatest poets. Growing up in a close-knit family in Amherst, Dickinson showed an early talent for writing and a keen interest in literature. Despite her reclusive nature and reluctance to seek publication, Dickinson's poems would later come to be celebrated for their profound insight, emotional depth, and innovative use of language.

Dickinson had an unconventional approach to poetry. Unlike many poets of her time, Dickinson eschewed traditional poetic forms and themes, opting instead for short, often enigmatic verses that explored themes of love, death, nature, and the human soul. Her distinctive style, characterized by dashes, unconventional punctuation, and vivid imagery, set her apart from her contemporaries and earned her a reputation as a visionary poet.

Dickinson's poems were largely unknown during her lifetime, with fewer than a dozen published anonymously. It wasn't until after her death in 1886 that her sister discovered hundreds of poems among her belongings. These poems, collected and published posthumously, revealed Dickinson's extraordinary talent and secured her place in the pantheon of American literature.

Despite her relative seclusion and the limited recognition she received during her lifetime, Dickinson's poetry would go on to exert a profound influence on subsequent generations of poets and writers. Her unique voice, daring experimentation, and profound insights into the human condition continue to captivate readers around the world, ensuring her legacy as one of the greatest poets in the English language.

Oliver Wendell Holmes

Oliver Wendell Holmes, born on March 8, 1841, in Boston, Massachusetts, emerged as one of the most influential jurists of the 20th century. Raised in a prominent family with strong literary and intellectual traditions, Holmes developed a keen intellect and a passion for law. After graduating from Harvard College and Harvard Law School, he embarked on a distinguished legal career that would leave a lasting impact on American jurisprudence.

An intriguing aspect of Holmes' life lies in his service during the Civil War. Despite initial reservations about the conflict, he enlisted in the Union Army and served as a lieutenant in several battles, including Antietam and Fredericksburg. Holmes' experiences on the battlefield profoundly influenced his worldview and shaped his ideas about the law and society.

Holmes' most enduring legacy stems from his tenure on the United States Supreme Court. Appointed by President Theodore Roosevelt in 1902, Holmes served on the Court for nearly three decades, earning a reputation as a staunch defender of free speech and civil liberties. His landmark opinions in cases such as Schenck v. United States and Abrams v. United States established a legal framework for interpreting the First Amendment and laid the groundwork for modern free speech jurisprudence.

Throughout his life, Holmes remained a towering figure in American law and letters. Known for his wit, intelligence, and incisive legal reasoning, he left an indelible mark on the legal profession and American society. Holmes' commitment to upholding constitutional principles and protecting individual freedoms continues to inspire generations of jurists and citizens alike.

Booker T. Washington

Booker T. Washington, born into slavery on April 5, 1856, in Hale's Ford, Virginia, rose to prominence as a leading educator, author, and civil rights leader. After the Civil War ended, Washington and his family gained their freedom, and he embarked on a quest for education. Despite facing numerous obstacles and challenges, including poverty and discrimination, Washington's determination led him to attend Hampton Normal and Agricultural Institute, where he honed his skills and developed a passion for teaching.

One interesting aspect of Washington's life is his famous "Atlanta Compromise" speech delivered in 1895. In this address, he urged African Americans to focus on economic advancement and vocational education rather than directly challenging Jim Crow laws and segregation. While controversial at the time, Washington's pragmatic approach earned him both praise and criticism from various quarters.

Washington's crowning achievement came with the founding of the Tuskegee Institute in 1881. Under his leadership, Tuskegee became a leading institution for African American education, emphasizing practical skills and self-reliance. Washington's philosophy of self-help and economic empowerment resonated with many in the African American community and helped pave the way for future generations of leaders.

Washington remained a tireless advocate for African American advancement and racial reconciliation for the rest of his life. Despite facing criticism from more radical voices within the civil rights movement, his efforts to promote education and economic self-sufficiency left an enduring legacy. Booker T. Washington's life serves as a testament to the power of perseverance, education, and leadership in the face of adversity.

4

Summary, and Further Reading

I hope you have enjoyed this work, because my team and I enjoyed assembling it for you.

The team at Daily Dose of Reason spent significant time and much debate selecting such an assortment of favorite lines, passages, and quotes from some of the Enlightenment minds that have had such a bearing on our lives.

If you liked the book, we would be honored if you leave a review. You can do it on Amazon, Goodreads, or wherever you like to leave book reviews.

Mailing List

If you are not yet on our mailing list and would like a weekly email containing an hand-picked quote and a quick education on the associated thinker and their life, please sign-up. Thousands receive it and give rave reviews.

Sign-up here: https://dailydoseofreason.ck.page/885fa387f7?

Made in the USA
Monee, IL
02 December 2024

71979046R00226